AF664250

Dedicated to
the soldiers of the Indian Army
who defend the world's most diverse Republic,
who give their today
for our peaceful tomorrow

Contents

Prologue

THE word "war" has been a subject of good tidings in all discussions all over the world nowadays. People, of all strata, groups, media, or states most powerful or weak, giant or tiny, are kept occupied with the word and its effects. War is a great human problem. The problem is that any human group or even the entire human race may be destroyed by an ultimate war at any moment. War is purely a human action. It is created, executed and justified by human beings. It is a curious paradox that though war is created by the action of men, it negates human values, morality and existence.

War is a brutal and ugly enterprise. Yet it remains central to human history and social change. These two facts together are paradoxical and inexplicable and they reveal a peculiar feature of human being, i.e. human beings have a tendency to dominate the others. The practical fact is that war and its threat continue to be forces in our lives. Recent world events like 9/11 attacks in USA, the counter-attack on Afghanistan, the overthrow of Iraq's Saddam Hussein, the Darfur crisis in Sudan, the bombings in Madrid and London, recent attacks of Britain, France and USA on Libya, and agitation in Egypt and the overthrow of president Hosni Mubarak prove this fact.

Wars are often the death knell of an old social order, the grim handmaidens for the birth of new ones. This process doesn't happen in a planned or systematic way on a political or ideological blueprint. The hallmark of war is chaos. War attacks the social fabric and brings loss of cohesion and fragmentation to systems and institutions that seemed solid and resistant to change in times of peace.

There are strong arguments in the opposite direction — that fundamental processes of social change may be interrupted but not changed in direction by war, that wars do not make fundamental changes in society, that the base is so strong that it cannot be changed by war.

War has diverse and seemingly contradictory effects on society. War has undercut socio-economic reforms, but it has also laid the basis for the modern welfare state.

There are people who believe that nations have to pursue their interests or defend themselves by war, if necessary, with the recognition that this will normally involve killing on a massive scale. At the other extreme there are those who, because they see killing as the ultimate wrong, regard war as entirely unacceptable. Between these two positions are those who feel the force of the pacifist's rejection of war, but who also see no alternative to war in certain extreme situations, and who are therefore morally torn. War is therefore one of the most deeply divisives of moral problems.

Philosophy is concerned with the life, specially human life — its values, nature, essence and justification. The issue of war naturally carries reflection on all these aspects of human life as war involves the question of life and death. War's violent nature and controversial social effect naturally raise some ethical problems and enquiry. Is war always wrong? Is there any situation when it can be justified? Will war always be part of human experience or can we do something to make it disappear? Is war an outcome of unchangeable human nature or of changeable social practice? Is there a fair and sensible way to wage war or is it a cruel and barbaric slaughter? At the end of war, how should post-war reconstruction proceed and who should be in-charge? What are our rights and responsibilities, when our own society makes the move to go to war? Hence, war demands philosophical inquiry and resolution quite naturally. As war is a human action, the search for its moral and rational justification, if there is any, is a pertinent issue of philosophy.

Philosophy is the true love for wisdom; wisdom is not devoid of human life and humanity. War, a supremely practical human activity, requires, naturally, a sound understanding in its full philosophical richness. As a matter of fact, if there is no philosophical contemplation upon war then the rules, codes and conduct of war will be purely arbitrary. Societies are more responsive now to the happenings around. War involves social life in multi-faceted way. Hence, a philosophical account of war is significant and it is a primary duty of service to humanity for the philosophy.

Every nation, people, community has its own way to meet real social issues. War is a real social issue in all ages. War plays a significant role in the context of the interrelation between two states. Both the Indian and Western philosophies have struggled with the problem of war since ancient times and how India and the Western world treat it in their own way needs ingenious exposition.

Since the ancient time war is an enduring reality of human life. Practically, war-reality has not been prevented by the cultural and progressive social development.

Most of the philosophers from the ancient time, while discussing war, express supportive, positive and defending attitude towards it. Reflecting on war issue from a general, theoretical approach the philosophers argue in favour of it as an instrument of social change; their justification for war involves warlike animal instinct of human beings, nature of the state power, i.e. the requirement of war to preserve freedom and sovereignty of a state and the affirmative contribution of war to the human world. They try to defend war from an altruistic view also, i.e. from the greatest happiness for the greatest number of people. Only in the recent times, chiefly in the twentieth century when nuclear war became a hard reality, philosophers raised their voice against the evil consequences of war.

Recent philosophical analysis of war attempts to resolve some issues. A very common argument in favour of war is that it preserves liberty and honour of a state. Presently, philosophy of war is trying to sort out that whether the preservation of such abstract values is more important than the preservation and progression of human civilization which faces a severe threat due to the conduct of war. Ancient philosophers justified war as it contributed — and promoted — to the human values. In the present scenario of nuclear war philosophers are engaged themselves with such a question — is war really preserve values? War is a conflict of values between two parties. When a state involves in a war for liberty and self-defence, the question arises that whether this war preserves individual's needs and values or personal values are considered secondary to the state machinery. In the past, war was defended as a cause for establishing justice. Present-day war philosophy raises the issue that whether justice can be achieved through the destruction and evil consequences of war, an empirical–practical reality.

Philosophical understanding of war involves a very basic issue, i.e. the origin of war which, again, reflects on the nature of war. Investigating the causes or the origin of war is significant as it is intimately concerned with the question of the elimination of war. If war originates from the essence of human nature then it is quite difficult to eliminate it. On the other hand, if war is caused by the social environment or condition then men can try to be free from the war.

Philosophical account of the causes of war may be viewed from sociological, biological and psychological aspects.

Marxist account of war is sociological as well as economical. It advocates that, the division of labour and the existence of private property divide a society into two conflicting classes. There is a constant struggle between these two classes as their interests are quite contrary to each other. This conflict between the classes leads to war among different states and nations. Conflicts of economic interest and the search for markets and raw materials contribute to the conduct of war. Sociological perspective of the causes of war hopes that the changes in the social and economic conditions may control and prevent war. In future, a classless society will be formed and then war will be a thing of the past.

According to the biological viewpoint, the origin of war lies in the very nature of man. Man possesses an animal instinct, an aggressive attitude and this instinct or attitude is quite conducive to war. War-instinct is a biological, natural and hereditary element of the human being and therefore, the elimination of war is an illusion or dream as the essence or nature of man is responsible for the origination of war. War springs from the minds of men — this is the main principle of the psychological view. It is evident that, man has self-love, desire for self-preservation. But he has a death-urge also. If he is not satisfied with his life then he may come to love death. This love for death attitude inspires him to get involved in war.

Till the first half of the twentieth century, practically, it is observed that war originated from the socio-economic sources. The society was divided into two classes, rich and the poor and the war was a conflict between them in which the rich section won as they were more powerful. Quite interestingly, concept of modern war has made a change to this aspect.

Modern war, with its new weapons, cannot confirm the victory of the rich like the earlier wars. Moreover, the role of religious issues is not presently so significant as the contribution to the conduct of war as it was in the past. Modern war, to some extent, contributes to the technological advancement. War strategy naturally demands modern, technically advanced weapons and consequently, there are new inventions in this field. Another thing is that, the nature of scientific research has changed due to the modern war system. In the present world, governments of almost all the countries have an increasing concern with the inventions of new, advanced weapons and a major part of the government finance is allotted to develop sophisticated weapons. As a result scientific research in this field is significantly dependent nowadays on the government policy and support. Scientists, involved in this type of invention procedure, are guided mainly by nationalistic approach; they are concerned with the security issue and interest of their own countries. So, neutral and disinterested attitude, which is essential for the pure scientific invention, is absent in this type of scientific research work. Moreover, this recent dependence of the science on the government gradually replaces individual investigation by the collective investigation process. Nowadays, scientists work collectively as a group under the government supervision and it raises a very significant question that whether creativity suffers due to this collective invention.

There is an intimate relation between war and international anarchy. This type of anarchy helps in breaking out war. Pragmatically, every state or nation forms its laws from the nationalistic outlook and if there is any international law or treaty which is not compatible with its self-interest then the nation prefers its own interest first and this type of attitude is quite conducive to war situation.

Again, war is a conflict of interests between two parties just like crime. Both crime and war spring from some conflict of interests and in both cases this conflict is tried to be solved by using force. If this sort of conflict is a natural disposition of human being then crime and war cannot be eliminated totally though they can be minimized; otherwise, socially or economically conditioned conflicts may be resolved without involving in crime and war.

War involves violence and it is a relationship between two or more states. This state aspect of war makes a distinction between war and other types of violence like terrorism, civil strife and national liberation movement.

It is the common notion that war is a continuous, unchanging social institution. But the social and economic conditions in which war breaks out have changed over time. To have a clear account of the nature, courses and causes of a particular war, it is necessary to have a clear understanding of the nature of the particular state and society in which the war has occurred. The relationship between the war and the society in which it is articulated and diffused is an important phenomenon in the context of the analysis of war nature. It is observed that with the changing nature of the states the war strategy or war policy has been changing and it is an obvious trend since the past several hundred years.

This intimate relation among war, state and society reflects on a very crucial, moral observation. Since the very past, political and social philosophers are remained concerned with the question of identity between state and society. This is a vital issue in the war discussion as it leads to an ethical question. The ethical problem is that, when a state is involved in a war with another state, then what will be the target of war — only the rival state or the entire society, i.e. non-combative population of that state. If state is different from the society then by no means the entire population will be the target of war as war is a relation between two states and not between the societies of those warring states. Hence, the issue of identification of the state and society is important as it is a deciding factor for the formation of certain rules for the waging of war.

There is another vital question regarding the relation between war and social change. The question is that whether war can be considered as an instrument of social change or it is a measure of social development. Some maintain the view that social and economic development, spread of industrialization are the causes which help in breaking out war and so, war is a measure of social and economic progression. On the other hand, there is another view which holds that war is a means to social development as it plays a remarkable role in the social, economic revolution.

War is a supremely practical human activity and so like all other human activities it is the subject to moral and ethical considerations and principles. It is generally assumed that war is a "last resort", i.e. for a state, war is the last ethical option. This observation needs critical moral and ethical analysis.

Regarding the rules of warfare, a question comes into mind that whether these rules should be theoretical or pragmatic, i.e. which one is more important — the establishment of theoretically consistent and coherent rules or the rules which can be followed in practical, empirical battlefield. This question arises as there is a gap between theory and practice, and consequently a confrontation between the two. It is a fact that we cannot question the theoretical or philosophical force of a principle or rule only because it is not followed in the practical field. Actually the rules of warfare intend to give a shape to the practice of waging war and it is not so much concerned with the actual happenings.

A sound and proper understanding of the concept of war demands reflections on all these philosophical issues which will explain nature and essence of war, its socio-economic and political aspects, and how moral and ethical concepts are related pragmatically to the issue of war.

1

Ancient Indian View on the Concept of War

THE ancient Indian thinkers distinctly discoursed on the theme of the nature of state and its management, both in the internal and external spheres. Concept of war is intimately related with the state management; war doctrine is a set of recurrent issues and themes in the discussion of state, hence, ancient Indian political treatises discussed war-issue as an integral part of the nature of state and its management. A state is not the only state in the world, hence, the interrelations of the states are also viewed critically as an important issue by the thinkers. As war plays a significant role in the context of inter-relation between two states, ancient Indian political discussions stressed on the different aspects of the war-issue.

R̥gveda, Purāṇas, *Rāmāyaṇa*, *Mahābhārata*, *Manu Saṁhitā*, *Arthaśāstra* and many other ancient Indian treatises have dealt interestingly with the question of war and they elaborately treated the pertinent issues of war.

The R̥gvedic Concept of War

In *R̥gveda*, hymns are dedicated to different gods. Hymns, which are predominantly concerned with Gods like Indra, Agni, Varuṇa and Pūṣan, reflect on the war-issue and a general philosophical orientation towards the subject.

Following hymns of *R̥gveda Saṁhitā* are devoted to God Indra.

purūtamaṁ purūṇāmiśānaṁ vāryāṇām ।
indraṁ some sacā sute ॥ — I.5.2

To him the richest of the rich, the lord of treasures excellent, Indra, will *soma* juice outpoured.

yasya saṁsthe na vṛṇvate harī samatsu śatravaḥ ।
tasmā indrāya gāyata ॥ — I.5.4

Whose pain of tawny horses yoked in battles foemen challenge not: To him, to Indra sing your song.

indra sānasiṁ rayiṁ sajitvānaṁ sadāsaham ।
varṣiṣṭhamūtaye bhara ॥ — I.8.1

Indra, bring wealth that gives delight, the victor's ever-conquering wealth, most excellent, to be our aid

ni yena muṣṭihatyayā ni vṛtrā ruṇadhāmahai ।
tvotāso nyarvatā ॥ — I.8.2

By means of which we may repel our foes in battle hand-to-hand, by thee assisted with the car.

indra tvotāsa ā vayaṁ vajraṁ ghanā dadīmahi ।
jayema saṁ yudhi spṛdhaḥ ॥ — I.8.3

Aided by thee, the thunder-armed Indra, may we lift up the bolt, and conquer all our foes in fight.

vayaṁ śūrebhirastṛbhirindra tvayā yujā vayam ।
sāsahyām pṛtanyataḥ ॥ — I.8.4

With thee, O Indra, for ally with missile-darting heroes, may we conquer our embattled foes.

mahām̐ indraḥ paraśca nu mahitvamastu vajriṇe ।
dyaurna prathinā śavaḥ ॥ — I.8.5

Mighty is Indra, yea supreme; greatness be his, the

Thunderer: wide as the heaven extends his power;

samohe vā ya āśata narastokasya sanitau |
viprāso vā dhiyāyavaḥ || — I.8.6

Which aideth those to win them sons, who come as heroes to the fight, or singers loving holy thoughts.

R̥gveda (I.11) states that Indra is a great hero and he has a great fighting-spirit; I.12 describes God Agni as the great oppressor of the foes.

Again, the hymns dedicated to both Indra and Varuṇa state:

indrāvarunayorahaṁ samrājorava ā vr̥ṇe |
tā no mr̥ḷāta īdr̥śe || — I.17.1

I crave help from the imperial lords, from Indra-Varuṇa; may they both favour one of us like me.

gantārā hi sthol 'vase havaṁ viprasya māvataḥ |
dhartārā carṣaṇīnām || — I.17.2

Guardians of men; ye ever come with ready succour at the call of every singer such as I.

anukāmaṁ tarpayethāmindrāvaruṇā rāya ā |
tā vāṁ nediṣṭhamīmahe || — I.17.3

State you, according to your wish, O Indra–Varuṇa, with wealth: Fain would we have you nearest us.

R̥gveda I.42 prays to God Pūṣan (sun god) in the following way:

ati naḥ saścato naya sugā naḥ supathā kr̥ṇu |
pūṣanniha kratuṁ vidaḥ ||7|| — I.42.7

Past all pursuers lead us, make pleasant our path and fair to tread. O Pūṣan, find thou power for this.

śagdhi pūrdhi pra yaṁsi ca śiśīhi prāsyudaram |
pūṣanniha kratuṁ vidaḥ ||9|| — I.42.9

Be gracious to us, fill us full, give, feel us, and invigorate: O Pūṣan, find thou power for this.

In all these hymns prayers are offered to different gods and these hymns repeatedly stress on the wealth, strength and power. These hymns seek God's grace for being affluent, strong, dynamic and vigorous. Gods are considered as the protectors of the subjects and a repeated emphasis is found on their energy, force, capability, assets, prosperity and the power of conquering the enemies. In the later period, *Manu Saṁhitā* and *Arthaśāstra* describe power, force and wealth as the qualities of an ideal king. For the protection of his state and subjects the king must try to suppress his enemy-state. Hence, this concept of the later Indian treatises actually originates from *R̥gveda*. Later Indian kings are mostly contemplated as the archetypal (representative) of God. Repeated prayers are offered to gods for acquiring prosperity and affluence by thrashing the hostile nation.

R̥gveda Saṁhitā I.73.10 prays to God Agni in the following manner:

etā te agna ucathāni vedho juṣṭāni santu manase hr̥de ca |
śakema rāyaḥ sudhuro yamaṁ te'dhi śravo devabhaktaṁ dadhānāḥ ||

May these our hymns of praise, Agni, ordainer, be pleasant to thee in thy heart and spirit.

May we have power to hold thy steeds of riches, laying on thee the God-sent gift of glory.

This hymn delineates that wealth or property eliminates poverty and the acquisition of wealth is again emphasized here. It is assumed that, *artha* (wealth) and *kāma* (desire) — two of the four *puruṣārtha*s of Indian tradition — are mentioned here. This hymn recognizes the significance of property and the desire to have it.

Here it should be remembered that this prayer is not offered directly by the king, but by the seers and the worshipper on whose behalf a brāhmaṇa performs religious rites; though it may be assumed that this hymn reveals the great value or importance of the ultimate desire of the human life of the Indian convention or belief which is applicable to all the *varṇas* (castes) of the ancient Indian society.

Again, *R̥gveda Saṁhitā* adores God Agni in this way:

> *uta bruvantu jantava udagnirvr̥trahājani* |
> *dhanañjayo raṇeraṇe* | — I.74.3

> And let men say, Agni is born, even he who slayeth Vr̥tra, he who winneth wealth in every fight.

Here, God Agni is worshipped as the conqueror of the enemy and by defeating the enemy wealth can be obtained.

> *agne naya supathā rāye asmānviśvāni deva vayunāni vidvān* || — I.189.1a

> By goodly paths lead us to riches, Agni, god who knowest every sacred duty.

This hymn stresses on the acquisition of property, but this collection of property should be fair and honourable.

R̥V I.190.5 indicates "Those, God, who count thee as a worthless bullock, and, wealthy sinners, live on thee the Bounteous."

In this case, God Br̥haspati is requested not to give asset or property to the evildoers or miscreants, i.e. it denotes that wealth must be fairly earned.

Once more,

supraitu sūyavaso sa panthā durniyantuḥ pariprīto na mitraḥ. . . ॥ — I.190.6

Those who unharmed by enemies behold us, while they would make them bare, stood closely compassed.

R̥gveda Saṁhitā, in this hymn, manifests that a king should restraint or repress the wrongdoers or mischievous, i.e. the subjugation of the wicked persons is a duty of an ideal king. God Br̥haspati is politely asked for to be a companion of the king who performs this duty.

From the above discussion it transpires that *R̥gveda* stresses on some issues which reveal the essence of war of the Indian tradition.

R̥gveda does not express complete disapproval of war. Instead of this, it indicates that war is indispensable in some situations. For the protection of the state and its subjects, and the acquisition of property, war is imperative and, here, war is for the welfare of the state. *R̥gveda* hymns explicitly stress on the power, strength and wealth, and this emphasis is not for the personal gain but for the well-being of the people and the state. Different gods are praised for their power and affluence, and their grace is repeatedly coveted for the attainment of strength and property. War is a means for the achievement of strength, power and wealth which are conducive to the conservation of the state and the society. *R̥gveda* approves war though this war should be right, fair and reasonable. Acquisition of property and power must be honourable and ethical. War is necessary for the repression of the enemies and this is also for the protection of the state. *R̥gveda* indicates that property can be obtained by defeating the enemy in war and this acquisition is conducive to the progression and development of the state as wealth eliminates poverty which is an obstacle for the formation of an ideal state. Wealth and proper management of property are indispensable for an ideal state. The essential quality of war as depicted in *Ṛgveda* is not at all aggressive in nature. *Ṛgveda* asserts that war is required for the attainment of power, strength and wealth, though all these are not for simply personal achievements but for the establishment and preservation of a balanced society and an ideal state. The acquisition of property is emphasized which is considered as one of the four *puruṣārtha*s or ultimate goals of human life of the Indian practice and this wealth is necessary for the welfare of the society and the state.

Purāṇas on War

Purāṇas, both the Mahāpurāṇas and Upapurāṇas, have dealt with the question of war and this discussion carries a reflection on the very essence of traditional Indian war-issue.

In *Śiva Purāṇa,* Nandikeśara says (chapter 6: 8-9):

> Arguing with each other (Viṣṇu and Brahmā) like this, saying that each is better than the other and claiming to be the Lord, they got ready to fight, like two foolish goats, desirous of killing each other.

Here, *Śiva Purāṇa* briefly states that, it will be a foolish task to be involved in a war only to show that one is superior than the other. It reveals that there must be some specific, genuine ground for war; it is not at all proper to take part in war due to some insignificant and contemptible issue.

In chapter 6, *śloka* 31 of *Śiva Purāṇa,* Īśvara (Śiva) says:

> O dear Hari, I am pleased with you, because you strictly adhered to truth in spite of you desire to be a Lord.

Śloka 33 says:

> Thus, the Lord was delighted by the truthfulness of Hari and offered him a footing equal to his own.

These *śloka*s point out that if someone has the desire to be a Lord, i.e. a powerful and strong person, he is expected also to be truthful and honest. One may aspire to be powerful and strong, but this craving must be fulfilled in a fair and candid way.

Again, chapter 9, *śloka* 26 of *Śiva Purāṇa* (*Rudra Saṁhitā*) describes the boasting of the king of demon (*asura*) Tāraka and the fight between him and Indra, Viṣṇu, Vīrabhadra. Here, Tāraka said about Viṣṇu that how can he (Viṣṇu) be considered an excellent, virtuous man, how can he be victorious in battle who has committed sin without caring for Vedic cult?

It denotes that honesty and fairness are required for attaining victory in the battlefield. If one tries to conquest an opponent in war he must be just and fair. Committing sin is not at all appropriate and relevant to a person desirous of victorious in a war.

Śiva Purāṇa (chapter 9, *śloka* 33), regarding the war between Kumāra and Tāraka, states that, on seeing the powerful *asura* (Tāraka) fallen dead in the battle, the hero (Kumāra) did not go and attack him again.

It shows that the combative warriors in the ancient India followed a high standard of morality and the ideal rules of war, in general, were quite ethical in nature.

Chapter 17 of *Śiva Purāṇa* gives an account of the fight between Viṣṇu and Jalandhara, the king of *asura*s. Here, Viṣṇu said to Jalandhara in the battlefield:

> Since you are a great Lord you are not at all afraid of even great weapons. I am delighted by this fight with you. You are really great. A hero like you has not been seen in the three worlds including the mobile and immobile beings.

Again, it indicates to the highly moral rules of war as depicted in the ancient Indian treatise. Jalandhara, one of the fighting warriors here, expresses admiration for the valour and heroism of the other warrior, Lord Viṣṇu. Admiring and glorifying the qualities of the opponent warrior refers to the magnanimity and generosity of the rules and nature of war in ancient India.

In chapter 22 of *Śiva-Purāṇa* Jalandhara, the king of *asuras*, tried to encourage his heroes in this way:

> To die cowardly while you profess to be heroes is not commendable, nor does it yield heaven.
>
> If you have faith in war or the essential strength in the heart or if you have no lurking pleasures for sexual indulgence then you come forward and stand before me.
>
> Death in battle is preferable. It yields all cherished desires. It is especially conducive to fame. It has been proclaimed as the bestower of salvation too.
>
> The wandering recluse of supreme knowledge and wisdom as well as he who dies fighting face-to-face, attain the greatest region after breaking through the solar sphere.
>
> No sensible man should ever be afraid of death.
>
> O heroes, death is congenital to any being born. Either today or at the end of 100 years, all living beings are sure to die.

Here, *Śiva Purāṇa* portrays the greatness or glory of war. To die heroic death in war field is praiseworthy and it is quite compatible with the eminence or fame. The warrior who dies in battlefield like a great hero ultimately attains the heaven. Death is an inevitable consequence for a living being and hence, no rational being should be afraid of it.

Umā Saṁhitā of *Śiva-Purāṇa* (chapter 21) states:

> A kṣatriya shall fight and get killed in battle for acquiring facilities to achieve the three aims of life (virtue, wealth and love) to all living beings or for the sake of cows and brāhmaṇa.

Again, in this case, *Śiva Purāṇa* expresses the magnificence (glory) of war. A kṣatriya or a warrior is expected to take part in a war for achieving *dharma*, *artha* and *kāma* (virtue, wealth and desire) which are the three *puruṣārtha*s or ultimate goals of human life of Indian tradition. So, war is conducive to the attainment of *puruṣārtha*s and not merely an aggressive matter.

Again, chapter 21 of *Śiva Purāṇa* describes — the hero who offers battle subduing the army of the enemy attains virtue, wealth and fame. He achieves the fruit of a sacrifice with due gifts and the three aims of life, virtue, wealth and love. He who faces the enemy, kills him and gets on to the enemy's chariot goes to Viṣṇuloka. He who is not defeated in war, nor killed in it attains the fruit of four horse sacrifices. He who dies in the war-front without surrendering his weapons attains heaven from which there is no return.

Those who die for the protection of cows, brāhmaṇa, status and the master go happily to the other world like virtuous persons.

A man may be competent to perform hundreds of sacrifices, but it is very difficult to renounce his own body in a righteous war. A righteous war is conducive to the attainment of heaven. It is sanctifying. It makes known the multi-faced beauty of a man.

Even a murderer shall not be attacked and killed if he is thirsty and begs for water.

One becomes a murderer of a brāhmaṇa by killing the sick, the feeble, the child, the hen-pecked, the miserly and one whose bow is broken.

After considering all these, an intelligent man shall strenuously indulge in battles. He will achieve the purpose of his life and rejoice here and hereafter.

Umā Saṁhitā, here, intimates that a warrior who brings under control the opponent force achieves three *puruṣārthas*, i.e. *dharma, artha, kāma* and the result of a sacrifice. A conqueror and a warrior who dies in the battlefield without surrendering his weapons attains heaven. He, who engages himself in war and die for the preservation and protection of his state and people goes to heaven like a virtuous person. *Śiva Purāṇa* delineates that the enjoyment of consequences of a righteous war is almost commensurate with the results of horse sacrifices. Here, the great respect and holiness of a righteous war is stressed on and such a war helps one to accomplish *puruṣārtha*s and heaven which are commonly attainable through performing sacrifices. Umā Saṁhitā clearly expresses that in a war a murderer who is thirsty, and those who are sick, weak, minor, miserly, whose bow is broken should not be attacked and killed. It refers to the highly moral rules of warfare and regard to general civil rights in ancient India.

An intelligent person is encouraged to be involved in a war as it will help him to achieve the purpose of his life.

Liṅga Purāṇa, in chapter 40, *śloka*s 50-53 states:

> King Pramiti will be born in the family of the Moon. He will have a big army. He will kill the *mleccha*s (alien outcaste people) in thousands. He will kill those who are not pious and virtuous.

Here, *Liṅga Purāṇa* reveals that it is a glorious and dignified matter for a king to suppress and kill those in a war who are not faithful and reverent. So, war is also a means to the preservation of social equilibrium and justice, as the evil and bad people may be punished and repressed through war.

In chapter 67, *śloka* 13, *Liṅga Purāṇa* describes:

> After conquering the earth including the seven islands and seven oceans, the son of Nahuṣa divided the kingdom into

> three parts among his sons. With the royal glory transferred to his sons and with the burden placed on his kins, the king became pleased.

In this context the following song was formerly sung by the great king Yayāti:

> A man shall be glorious if only he withdraws all his desires like the tortoise withdrawing all its limbs; otherwise not, even if he performs a crore of holy rites.

In this *śloka*, *Liṅga Purāṇa* denotes that desires and passions should be controlled and it helps one to be pleasurable and magnificent. This is true not for only common people but also for the rulers and warriors. Performance of rituals and rites cannot bear proper results if desires are not regulated. This restraint and administration of desires is quite relevant in the context of war for a king.

War-issues, as depicted in the Purāṇas, show some significant features of the Indian view. Ancient Indian authorities emphasize on the real and genuine ground for war, trustfulness and honesty of a warrior to become strong, powerful and victor; highly ethical rules of warfare and a fair and just attitude towards the defeating people. Heroic death in the battlefield is stressed on and righteous war is viewed as the means to the attainment of heaven and *puruṣārthas*. A king must involve in a war for the protection of his state and people. So, Purāṇas declare the glory of war which is ethical and hence, non-aggressive in nature.

War in Rāmāyaṇa Prespective

Rāmāyaṇa, the great Indian epic and ancient Indian treatise on social, political, ethical issues, distinctly describes state as *saptāṅga* (made of seven parts) — *rājan* (king), *amātya* (minister), *janapada* (country), *durga* (fort), *koṣa* (treasury), *daṇḍa* (army) and *suhṛd* (friend), and *daṇḍa* as an imperative, crucial and vital element of the state. Being an inevitable part of the state management, *daṇḍa* obviously delineates war as an eloquent issue for the proper administration and management of the state.

Following the Indian tradition, *Rāmāyaṇa* reveals that protection and maintenance of the state and its subjects is the crucial and prime duty of a king or kṣatriya. Ādi-Kāṇḍa of *Rāmāyaṇa* points out that King Hariścandra and King Aja are the great kings and they protect and preserve the people of their states as their own sons. To repress the evil elements, waging war is necessary for the safety and security of the society and the state. Ādi-Kāṇḍa states that to suppress and kill the demon Rāvaṇa, God Nārāyaṇa will be born in Ayodhyā as Rāma. The war between Rāma and Rāvaṇa is a war between good and evil elements, and the defeat of Rāvaṇa is absolutely required for the preservation of social morality and equilibrium.

Again, in Ādi-Kāṇḍa, we find that Saṁvara, a demon (*asura*) defeated God Indra and occupied his kingdom, i.e. heaven (*svarga*). Then, King Daśaratha of Ayodhyā received a request from Indra, and the king suppressed and killed Saṁvara. This is also a clash or combat between fair and atrocious, impious elements. Ādi-Kāṇḍa describes that in the state of Mithilā the sages could not perform sacrifices due to the oppression and outrage from the demons, mainly from Mārīca. Hence, the great sage Viśvāmitra requested King Daśaratha to give permission to Rāma and Lakṣmaṇa to kill the demons and ultimately these demons were outraged by the two great brothers, Rāma and Lakṣmaṇa. In Uttara-Kāṇḍa Rāmacandra tells the great sage Agastya that in Laṅkāwar innumerable number of *rākṣasa* (demons), who were great heroes were killed by Lakṣmaṇa and himself. So, it is a matter of pride for an ideal ruler to conquer the immoral ones. It is considered as *kṣātra-dharma* or *rāja-dharma* for a king to be involved in a war for the protection of his country and subjects.

Ādi-Kāṇḍa portrays a conflict between King Daśaratha of Ayodhyā and the God Indra. Due to drought or want of rain for fourteen years people of Ayodhyā were suffering terribly, and to save and secure his own subjects King Daśaratha conducted an expedition against Indra, the God of Rain.

Moreover, a king should try to expand his territories by acquiring other lands or countries. This is also for the welfare of his state. Expansion of the territory helps in the augmentation of power and prosperity of the king, and a resourceful and cogent ruler can discharge his duties more perfectly and efficiently. Ādi-Kāṇḍa gives a detailed account of *aśvamedha yajña* performed by the King Dilīpa of Ayodhyā. Dilīpa appointed his son Raghu as the protector of the horse of the said sacrifice and to conquer the other territories. Uttara-Kāṇḍa indicates that great Rāmacandra also performed *aśvamedha yajña*. In ancient days Indian kings and rulers who were great heroes used to perform *aśvamedha yajña* which was a means to expand their territories and consequently their power, assets and sovereignty.

Again, a rich treasure (*artha*) and affluence is required for the formation of an ideal state and society. It makes the ruler more powerful to protect his country and hence, for the felicity and well-being of the state, a king must try to possess a rich treasure. Collecting revenues from the enemy nations with which he is in war can help the king to augment his prosperity.

An ideal king must have the desire to conquer and become a powerful and efficient king for the development and progression of his state and people.

Rāmāyaṇa views the war from the perspective of the fulfilment or attainment of *trivarga* (three of the four *puruṣārthas* or ultimate goals of human life advocated by the Indian authorities), i.e. *dharma, artha* and *kāma* which consequently lead to the prosperity of the nation.

War is conducive to the advancement and progression of the state; *Rāmāyaṇa* reveals that war helps the ruler to attain *dharma, artha* and *kāma*. But at the same time, this great epic is of the opinion that conflict should be considered as the last resort. It views the very practical and empirical perspectives of war and, hence, contemplates on the immediate effects of war which lead to the loss of people and money. *Rāmāyaṇa* suggests the king to try to avoid war by *sāma, dāna* and *bheda* principles first and if all these fail, then war is to be waged. Laṅkā-Kāṇḍa of *Rāmāyaṇa,* shows that before the war great Rāma sent Aṅgada as his messenger to the royal court of Rāvaṇa and Aṅgada tried to pursue Rāvaṇa to agree to restore/ return Devī Sītā to Rāmacandra. But Rāvaṇa did not agree and, hence, war was an inevitable and destined outcome.

Like the other Indian treatise, *Rāmāyaṇa* lays down some rules of warfare which delineate its preference towards the ethical and non-aggressive nature of war. This epic holds that it is not a sin to kill one who has struck first, for one has to save one's life as best one can. But even in war one must not kill an enemy who is not fighting, has taken to hiding or sought refuge with folded hands, is running away or drunken. Kiṣkindhā-Kāṇḍa gives an account of the war between Rāma and Bāli, the monkey-king of Kiṣkindhā. Rāmacandra killed Bāli not in open fight but he remained in concealment and killed Bāli. In ancient days this was not a proper and ethical rule of war and so, Bāli, in his death-bed and Tārā, the wife of Bāli, reproached Rāma to be involved in such a war. Hence, open or face-to-face fight was more praiseworthy or laudable than a concealed-war. Again, King Bāli rebuked Rāmacandra on the ground that he killed him without any serious offence. To kill someone without any guilt/crime and deceitfulness in war was highly reprehensible. Rāma was also reproved by Bāli for his involvement in a crafty/

fraudulent war as it was an impious task; war should not be devoid of virtue or righteousness (*dharma*).

In *Rāmāyaṇa*, we find highly ethical post-war attitude towards the conquered nation and people. In Laṅkā-Kāṇḍa, Mandodarī, the wife of King Rāvaṇa, overwhelmed with sorrow, was given assurance of security, protection and encouragement by Rāmacandra after the death of Rāvaṇa. Again, great Rāma gave the instruction to Vibhiṣaṇa to perform the obsequies of Rāvaṇa and the other heroes of Laṅkā in a proper way and the cremation was performed by Vibhiṣaṇa, Hanumān and the other monkey-battalion in a royal manner. After this, Vibhiṣaṇa was bathed with consecrated water and was crowned as the king of Laṅkā by Rāmacandra. All these post-war attitudes point out that the defeated king and his soldiers should be honoured and the protection, reconstruction and progression of the conquered state is the responsibility of the victor king. Readiness to fight, expedition, end of a war and victory will be of good fame and illustrious if it is imitated by a moral and ethical post-war attitude of the conquered nation.

Rāmāyaṇa reveals that war should be raised as the last recourse or option when it appears necessary for the maintenance of social justice, social equilibrium and development of the nation. As this war is the last resort, it is *dharma-yuddha*, the non-occurrence of which dismantles and abolishes social peace and stability. Rules of war and post-war attitude towards defeated enemies in *Rāmāyaṇa* clearly depicts non-antagonistic, non-offensive and moral attitude of war; war is for the welfare of the state management and not for any personal aggression. Valour, courage and heroism are praised through the entire *Rāmāyaṇa*, and this valour is conducive to the attainment of *trivarga* and the progression and prosperity of the state.

Concept of War in Mahābhārata

Mahābhārata distinctly discoursed on the theme of the nature of state and its management; both in the internal and external spheres it included *daṇḍa* as an indispensable part of the state. The state, according to it, constituted by *saptāṅga*, one of which is *daṇḍa*.

During the conversation between Bhīṣma and Yudhiṣṭhira in Śānti-Parva of *Mahābhārata* Bhīṣma asserts that a state has seven distinct elements (*saptāṅga*) in it, namely the king, the minister, the country, the fort-capital, the treasury, *daṇḍa* and *suhr̥d*. According to this exposition all the elements are interdependent.

So, it was considered that *daṇḍa* happened to be an integral part of the state; without *daṇḍa* waging of war could never be possible and a state without *daṇḍa* suffered to have no sovereignty, i.e. it would be incomplete in maintaining the said *saptāṅga*.

Śānti-Parva of *Mahābhārata*, explicitly states that, charity, performance of sacrifice, study and the protection of the subjects are the duties of a kṣatriya. Waging war against the evil elements or assailant is the prime duty of a king just as the study, teaching, officiating on sacrifices performed for others are the foremost duties of the brāhmaṇas. A person, may be, a friend or a teacher (*guru*), if becomes a threat to *saptāṅga* of a state, must be confronted resolutely, if necessary, by the king in the battlefield. Involvement in a war for the protection of the country makes the kṣatriya behaving in a way that is right. In Śānti-Parva Draupadi says to Yudhiṣṭhira that a powerless person can never be able to enjoy the wealth and the lands of this world and hence his subjects are also deprived of enjoying it. Friendship and charity to everyone may be considered as the duties of brāhmaṇas, but not of kṣatriyas. Repression of the evil ones, protection of the honest and good people, and the involvement in war, when required, are the prime duties of a king.

Again, Arjuna says to Yudhiṣṭhira that heroism or valour is always praiseworthy. Those gods who have repressed the demons are worshipped by the people. Rudra, Kārttikeya, Indra, Agni, Varuṇa, Yama, Kāla, Kubera, Sūrya, Marut, Vasu are those gods who are adored for their valour.

So, in case of the assaults by the invaders causing serious threat to the integrity and security of the country, waging of war against the invaders was considered as *kṣātra-dharma*. The observance of the duty causes good to the king. The theory of *āpad-dharma* (expediency), no doubt which lays down a practical course of conduct, not usually proper but allowable in times of extreme necessity or distress, shows that the idea of virtue and vice was admitted to be relative and dependent on circumstances. But at the same time, cardinal virtues and fundamental vices are recognized in accordance with the general trend of traditional piety.

Regarding the conquest of a new territory, in Śānti-Parva, Bhīṣma holds the view that to have in possession unacquired lands forms a part of king's duty. This, together with the duty to protect the acquired ones, do good to his subjects. A king needs to engage himself to succeed righteously in a battle and to add riches to his treasure. A king who wants to acquire *dharma,* i.e. who is *dharmārthī* requires to be engaged in wars to acquire treasure so that being resourceful and stable he can serve better to enrich his subjects. Possession of a rich treasure collected from his own and the other countries, forms a duty for a king. A rich treasure happens to be a coefficient factor to manage other five *aṅga*s of state leading to prosperity and stability, thus it leads to social *dharma*. For the protection of the subjects a rich treasure is required. A kṣatriya or a king should have the desire to conquer and have wealth.

Arrangement for proper defensive measures of his country and the people is the prime task of the king and to accomplish this prime duty, the king, if necessary, may project himself or his strategies in deferring projections like a peacock. A simile is attributed here, a peacock under sunbeam reflects as if it has different shades. The king has to consider the variety of situations and according to those he has to mend his courses of actions. If required, he has to prevail over his enemies and acquire wealth from other countries.

In the traditional Indian thought four *puruṣārtha*s or ultimate goals of our lives are admitted. But the highest goal (*mokṣa*) is not generally recommended for the householder. *Dharma, artha* and *kāma* are the *trivarga*s which are observable by them and so, a king, being a householder, must pursue *trivarga* in his life.

To observe his *kṣātra-dharma* or *rāja-dharma* the king has to protect not only his country and subjects from the invaders/ assaulters but he has to occupy or conquer other territories, *prajā-pālana* and *rājya-rakṣā,* i.e. the prime duty of a king makes him involved in both these elements. In the face of a foreign invasion a defensive war becomes an unavoidable necessity, its avoidance leads not only to the sacrifice of all that is worthwhile, but also defeats the very purpose for which war is desired to be avoided. Again, a king should try to augment his capability and force, since a king who is powerless can't save his country. It is obvious that having control over larger territories a king generally becomes powerful to protect his subjects properly. The observance of his *rāja-dharma* sincerely and honestly is necessary for a king because when *dharma* suffers, everything is destroyed. So, due to *kṣātra-dharma* or *rāja-dharma* a king should be in a defensive war against the invaders. In addition to this, a *vijīgīṣu* (one desirous of fresh conquest) king is also expected to be in non-defensive war because such extension of territories by an efficient king that upholds *rāja-dharma* properly ushers to auspicious good to the extended territories.

In *Bhagavad-Gītā* Lord Kṛṣṇa, exhorts Arjuna to fight against his relatives and kins, as, being a kṣatriya, he must follow his *sva-dharma* of fighting those who stood in the battlefield as his enemies. Everyone has been assigned certain duties by virtue of being placed in the world with a certain status in life and he has to perform his assigned duties (*sva-dharma*). Otherwise the society will be ruined. So, a king, being the saviour and protector of his country, must observe his *sva-dharma,* i.e. *prajā-pālana, rājya-rakṣā* and involve himself in war for the sake of these two.

Mahābhārata repeatedly emphasize on the augmentation of wealth of the king. As without a rich treasure a king can't be powerful and without possessing considerable power he can't save his country, so, for the protection of his subjects which is the *rāja-dharma* a king must have efforts to have a rich treasure. Besides collecting taxes from his own country he can also increase wealth having those from other states engaged in war.

Again, *Mahābhārata* holds that a king should have the quality of becoming *vijīgīṣu*. A king's desire (*kāma*) to conquer and become a sovereign should be viewed in its right perspective. *Rāja-dharma* involves this type of desire as it is essential for the protection, prosperity and development of the state. A powerless king without the desire to increase his power and treasure can't govern and protect his kingdom. The desire to augment treasure, power and friend, collecting taxes and revenue from other territories as well as from own state makes a king prosperous and powerful. So, a king who wants to discharge his duties properly by making his state powerful and prosperous should possess the desire to protect his people from exterior aggression first and then, being desirous of becoming a sovereign, may wage a war on other lands.

Mahābhārata holds the question of war in this perspective and have not segregated it from the observance of *rāja-dharma*. Thus it is linked to the attainment of *trivarga*.

In spite of the opinion that war is a part of *rāja-dharma* and it helps the king in the attainment of *trivarga*, *Mahābhārata* also expresses the opinion that a *vijīgīṣu* king should first try to possess his enemies through the three-fold methods of *sāma*, *dāna* and *bheda*. The ruler has to try to influence and conquer his enemies by the means of establishing close and intimate relation with them, giving suggestions, discussions with each other (*sāma nīti*), giving money and other valuable gifts to them (*dāna nīti*) and creating a division among the enemies (*bheda nīti*). When all these principles fall in vain the king has to wage a war.

Here, *Mahābhārata* expresses a very pragmatic view. War is found to have a base in reality for the protection and prosperity of the state. But the state suffers from loss of people and money as an immediate effect of a war. On the other hand, victory in a war is not certain at all. So, *Mahābhārata* suggests to try to possess new territories through *sāma, dāna, bheda* principles first; and when those methods are exhausted, then the king may seek option in war. Progress and prosperity should be the aim of a king. If that goal is achieved by avoiding war, that should be done. War, as such, is considered as a means of last resort.

Mahābhārata suggests some principles of warfare which should be followed by the kṣatriyas or kings. It holds the view that an old man, a mere boy, a woman, one who has surrendered with the words "I am yours", who is asleep, who has withdrawn from contest, who is disarmed, who is a mere spectator, who is mourning the loss of his son, whose body is charged with the enemy's arrows, who is afraid, one who is thirsty, fatigued, taking food and drink, fatally wounded are not to be killed. One must fight only with one person at a time. One who is on horseback should not rush towards one who is seated on a chariot, one who is seated on a chariot can rush towards another charioteer. When other party wants to surrender the king must stop the war.

Above all, *Mahābhārata* makes the codification of war laws on human rights and tried to keep war principles out of savage malice as war is considered as a part of social reality and the kings are advised not to take part in unjust war. A just war is permissible. It is far better to die in a righteous or just war than winning in an unjust war, for a king can never win fame by achieving victory following unrighteous means in the battlefield.

Besides the rules of warfare, post-war attitude of the victor king towards the conquered enemies, i.e. the steps by which conquered territory is to be pacified and normal life restored in it are also discussed in *Mahābhārata*.

In Śānti-Parva, Bhīṣma says Yudhiṣṭhira that, as the war brings sufferings and hardships to the subjects of the states involved in the war, a king, after winning a war, must involve himself in the protection, reconstruction and development of the conquered land as means to bring the people of that land to control.

Mahābhārata finds the significance of war in the maintenance of power, potential and affluence of the state, and the protection and conservation of its subjects. For the fulfilment of *trivarga*, war is a necessity for a king and the state. But at the same time, *Mahābhārata* also makes a distinction between *dharma-yuddha* and *adharma-yuddha* and it clearly shows its preference towards *dharma-yuddha*. *Dharma-yuddha* is conducive to the attainment of *trivarga* and the betterment and furtherance of the state. When the other policies (*sāma, dāna, bheda*) break down and diminish, then only the king should engage in war and so war is the last resort and consequently it is *dharma-yuddha*. Such a war is indispensable for if a king does not take part in it, the society will suffer. War is for the safety and security of the state and society, and not for any personal advantage and interest. Hence, war is not antagonistic and aggressive in nature. Moreover, rules of war and post-war attitude towards the conquered people as recommended by the War Concept in *Mahābhārata* reveal a highly ethical perspective, and non-aggressive approach and aspect of the ancient India.

War Concept in Manu Saṁhitā (Manusmr̥ti)

Manu Saṁhitā, the most important and effective Dharmaśāstra of the social life in India, holds that a state is not the only state in the world; hence, the interrelation of the states is viewed critically as an important issue by it. War, being a significant aspect in the context of interrelation between two states, is stressed on by the ancient treatise and it includes *daṇḍa* as a part of *saptāṅga* of the state. *Manu Saṁhitā* states that state comprises *svāmī* (king), *amātya* (minister), *pura* and *durga* (country and fort), *koṣa* (treasury), *daṇḍa* (army) and *suhr̥d* (friend).

Manu, following Indian tradition, i.e. Vedas, determines in his famous *Manu Saṁhitā* the respective duties of the four castes — brāhmaṇas, kṣatriyas, vaiśyas and śūdras. He holds that the duty of a kṣatriya or a king who is the chief *aṅga* (limb) of the seven elements of a state is the protection of the lives of his subjects from internal–external unrest and exploits, giving gifts, performance of sacrifice, study and the non-attachment to the worldly pleasures such as dancing, singing, woman, etc. Of all these specific duties protection of his subjects is the chief duty of a king or kṣatriya.

Due to this *prajā-pālana,* i.e. the protection of his *prajā* or subjects a king has to be involved in a war. If his state or country is so attacked that it threatens the security and the lives of his subjects then he must wage a war to defeat the invader. The invader, in such case, is an *ātatāyī* and the king has to defend his state and wipe out, if so required, the *ātatāyī* without any other consideration.

So, for the protection of the state and people, waging war on the invaders and the efforts to win over them is an obligatory duty for a kṣatriya or a king as this brings auspicious good to the king.

Hence, when the state is assaulted by the invaders which causes threat to the unity and safety of the state, to be involved in a war against those invaders is *rāja-dharma* (royal duty of a king). The accurate and proper performance of such duty helps the king to acquire good consequence in his life.

In the question of annexation and subjugation of a new region *Manu Saṁhitā* says that a king must involve himself into the occupation of unacquired lands and try to safeguard possession over those lands (*janapada*) by constant efforts.

Again the king has to try to acquire the unacquired lands with *daṇḍa,* i.e. with the army (elephants, horses, chariots and foot-soldiers) and for the attainment of *puruṣārtha*s, i.e. the cherished goals of our temporal lives obtaining the new lands and their protection are necessary or obligatory and the king should remain ever active to do so.

Manu is of the opinion that a king may be coarse in one case and tender in another. A king should have the single-minded patience of a crane while pondering over the attainment of other kingdoms. The king needs to maintain the preparedness of his army for possible battle.

It is a sacred royal duty for a king to safeguard his state and people from the external aggression and also to try to possess new domains or lands. *Prajā-pālana* or *rājya-rakṣā*, the prime duty of the king, may be observed through war and conquering new states. Protective or defensive war in the case of foreign attack is obligatory, otherwise it will destroy all that is worthwhile. To be a powerful king, which is essential for the advancement and development of a nation, the ruler must try to conquer new territories. A sincere and honest effort from the part of the king for the observance of his *rāja-dharma* is necessary as when *dharma* suffers, everything is destroyed. Manu says, "*Dharma* being violated, destroys; *dharma* being preserved, preserves" (Manu viii.15). Hence, for the *kṣātra-dharma* or *rāja-dharma* protective as well as non-defensive war is required for a king to make his state good, advanced and prosperous.

Manu Saṁhitā again and again stresses on the intensifying and magnifying of the wealth of the ruler. An opulent (rich) and sumptuous treasure makes a king powerful which consequently helps in the proper protection and management of the state and society. The king may possess a rich treasure by collecting taxes from his own people and from the other states with which he subdued in war.

Manu Saṁhitā also points out that a king should be a *vijīgīṣu*. Hence, Manu considers the question of war as a means to achieve *dharma, artha* and *kāma,* i.e. *trivarga* for the king and his kingdom.

It is mentionable that though war is advantageous and contributes towards the attainment of *trivarga* and the observance of *rāja-dharma, Manu Saṁhitā* clearly opines that war is the last choice or last course of action. The ruler should follow the principles of *sāma, dāna* and *bheda* first to conquer his enemies and new territories, and when all these fail he has to apply *daṇḍa-nīti*. Among the four, Manu praises the principles of *sāma* and *daṇḍa* for the protection and development of the state because if *sāma-nīti* is pursued then there is no preparation for war, loss of property or wealth and people (army). On the other hand, though the application of *daṇḍa-nīti* causes all these but ultimately it leads to the good of the state. Both the principles — *sāma* and *daṇḍa* — are for the well-being of the state and society; but from the pragmatic point of view Manu prefers *sāma-nīti,* imitating or following of which helps in the avoidance of loss of people and asset, and we cannot refrain from all the immediate effects of war in the pursuance of *daṇḍa-nīti.*

In the course of discussion of war in *Manu Saṁhitā* some rules of warfare are proposed for the king or ruler. This great ancient treatise holds that a king should not apply any *kūṭastra* or *guptī,* i.e. any sword or knife kept concealed in the war. Moreover, a king should avoid the use of any poisoned weapon and the weapon which is heated in the battlefront. Again, one should fight only with one person at a time. One who is on a chariot should not discharge weapon towards the infantry. An old man, a mere boy, a woman, one who has surrendered with the words "I am yours", who is asleep, who has withdrawn from contest, who is disarmed, who is a mere spectator, who is mourning the loss of his son, whose body is charged with the enemy's arrows, who is afraid, one who is thirsty, fatigued, taking food and drink, fatally wounded are not to be killed. The soldier who is aversed to war due to fear or dread and is killed by his opponent is sharing the sin of his master, i.e. king. Manu opines that it is not possible and even fair that one (the soldier) is enjoying the fruit of the action of another person (the king). *Manu Saṁhitā* indicates that one who attains victory in a war and possesses chariot, horse, elephant, umbrella, animals, treasure, grain, female servant, salt, carpet or mat, copper-vessel from the defeated country, is the real master of all these things. These rules of war are, no doubt, ethical in nature.

The aforesaid thinker engaged himself to codify the war-laws having consideration on human rights and tried to keep war principles out of savage malice as war was considered as a part of social reality. The kings were advised not to take part in unjust war. A just war was permissible. It is far better to die in a righteous or just war than winning in an unjust war, for a king can never gain fame having victory following unrighteous means in the battlefield.

Ancient Indian treatises also elaborately discuss post-war attitude of the victor or the triumphant king towards the conquered nation and say that the restoration of the normal life, the protection of the conquered people and the distribution of acquired property among the people of the land are the duties of the victor king. Manu expresses the view that after achieving victory over the opponents the conqueror has to worship brāhmaṇas and gods of the conquered land, repair the damaged temples (if any), reduce the payable taxes of the conquered people, gift a part of the acquired property in a war to them and protect them.

Manu Saṁhitā delineates the view that the king or the ruler can attain *trivarga* through his involvement in a war for the sake of the welfare of his state and people. *Rāja-dharma* inspires and obligates the king to be engaged in a war which makes his state progressive, pioneering and wealthy. In spite of his opinion that war is for the advancement of the state Manu does not ignore the very pragmatic aspect that the biggest casualty of war is the innocent and to avoid this he proposes war as the last option. Rules of war and post-war attitude in *Manu Saṁhitā* show respect and admiration towards human life, human value and dignity. It is *rāja-dharma* of a king to safeguard his own state and people, and for this to be engaged in a war. But equally, at the same time, the king is advised to show reverence and honour towards life, value and dignity of the individuals of the other state with which he is in war.

Interpretation of War in the Arthaśāstra

Arthaśāstra of Kauṭilya, another great ancient Indian treatise, deals interestingly with the question of war. Kauṭilya asserts the importance of war in the management of state.

The state, according to this great thinker, is constituted by *saptāṅga,* one of which is *daṇḍa. Arthaśāstra* states that the elements which form the state are *rājan* (king), *amātya* (minister), *janapada* (country), *durga* (fort), *koṣa* (treasury), *daṇḍa* (army) and *suhṛd* (friend).

Kauṭilya views the question of war from the angle of peace (*śānti*) and industry (*vyāyāma*). His arguments are advanced basically from the economic aspects of the people within the kingdom and society. To him, industry means effort to achieve the results of works undertaken and peace denoted, in this case, absence of disturbance to the enjoyment of the results achieved from works. This argument is initiated because acquisition and security of property are dependent upon peace and industry. As no society could survive (and thereby prosper also) without the acquisition and security of property — as no society could be said to have civility without this security — the unhindered maintenance of industry and peace are considered the prime necessity of a stable society.

Kauṭilya's prime consideration is about the three aspects of position of the state — deterioration, stagnation and progress. To him, the causes of human make which uses to affect position are policy and impolicy (*naya* and *apanaya*). Fortune and misfortune (*aya* and *anaya*) are providential causes. *Arthaśāstra* holds the view that both the human and providential causes govern and control all the affairs of this world.

He further opines that what is anticipated is human and the attainment of a desired end as anticipated is due to the policy followed. The policies that produce unfavourable results are impolicy and those producing favourable results are good policy. In his opinion for the progress of the state sixfold policies are good — peace (*sandhi*), war (*vigraha*), observance of neutrality (*asana*), marching (*yāna*), alliance (*samāśraya*) and making peace with one and waging war with another. Of these, agreement with pledge is peace; offensive operation is war; indifference is neutrality; making preparations is marching; seeking the protection of another is alliance; and making peace with one and waging war with another is termed a double policy. These sixfold policies are the proper policies to determine the progress of the state; progress of the state again dependent on peace and industry. The sixfold policies are necessary because of the existence of many states. Existence of many states is a reality and war between states is an impending possibility which would cause the strife in the public life disturbing the stability and good endeavour for works in a society. That would mean deterioration or stagnation of social condition in a state. Considering this aspect Kauṭilya delineates the proper policy of war in his sixfold policies. Thus the circle of states is the source of sixfold policies.

Kauṭilya also categorizes the states into three groups: powerful, equally powerful with others and weak from the others. According to him, states should follow strategies out of these sixfold policies in accordance with their own positions. If the state is powerful it might have considered of launching a *vigraha* on the comparatively weaker neighbour for its own extension. The weaker state, on the other hand, should have followed the policy of *sandhi* to protect his own interest from the powerful neighbouring state. Two equally powerful states should have needed to observe a policy of *asana* to protect their respective interests. Similarly, *yāna*, *samāśraya* and making peace with one and waging war with another should have been followed in accordance with the convenience and necessities of the state. All these systematic arguments are advanced to maintain the proper condition in the society for acquisition and security of property that are dependent upon peace and industry.

Kauṭilya's main stress is on the economic aspect of the society because in his conception progress of a society is dependent on the economic and intellectual prosperity of the society. This is, *inter alia*, connected with the source of sovereign states argued by Kauṭilya in *Arthaśāstra*. He points to the king, the minister, the country, the fort, the treasury, the army, the friend and the enemy as the elements of sovereignty. An analysis will show that all these elements are involved with the sixfold policies for the determination of deterioration, stagnation and progress of state. Therefore, in his view the question of peace and industry involves with the elements of sovereignty. This is a very important aspect of Kauṭilya's *Arthaśāstra*. He states that sovereignty of a state could not be maintained without a proper policy because impolicy could not maintain peace and industry where a state is in the circle of states. Another important aspect emerges from this argument — as he has categorized three aspects of states — that war is caused ultimately by desire. This desire again is based on economic grounds because no desire in the real political world is without a desire for gain, i.e. it is essentially of economic character. From this angle of vision Kauṭilya enlarges the economic interpretation of the source of war.

Kauṭilya relates the issue of war with the sovereignty of the state (kingdom) and while discussing the same he defines the terms conqueror, enemy — natural enemy and factitious enemy, etc. His definitions are specific and special.

Arthaśāstra states:

> The king who, being possessed of good character and best fitted elements of sovereignty, is the fountain of policy, is termed the conqueror.

Again,

> the king who is situated anywhere immediately on the circumference of the conqueror's territory is termed the enemy.

And

> that foe who is equally of high birth and occupies a territory close to that of the conqueror is a natural enemy; while he who is merely antagonistic and creates enemies to the conqueror is a factitious enemy.

All these definitions are related with the question of prosperity of the state and Kauṭilya is also thoughtful about the neighbouring states, i.e. he stresses on the question of circle of states.

Proceeding from these premises Kauṭilya mentions three kinds of strength and three kinds of happiness which led him to a theorem: "Strength is power and happiness is the end." He categorizes the three kinds of strength in this way — power of deliberation is intellectual strength; the strength of sovereignty is the passion of a rich, prosperous treasury and a powerful army; and the material power is physical strength.

And in respect of three kinds of happiness he opines that the end which is attainable by deliberation is the end of deliberation; the end of sovereignty is attainable by the strength of sovereignty and that end which is attainable by the preservation is the end of martial power.

This strength and happiness are not the strength and happiness of a single individual or a group of people, but are of the entire state (kingdom) because the three elements (kinds) that formed the "strength" are intellectual, martial and material powers. He conceives that the absence of any one of these elements, i.e. intellectual strength (education and higher proficiency of scholarship), prosperous treasury, i.e.

strong economic position, and physical strength, i.e. strong martial power, means the incompetence of "strength" of the state. In other words, only the combination of these three could mean the real strength of the state and this strength is indispensable for the maintenance of sovereignty. And, by the next rational approach, the end deliberation of the three is happiness as he states "happiness is the end".

Kauṭilya's entire discussion on war is invariably in the perspective of welfare of the state (kingdom). He doesn't dismiss the necessity of war; he is a pragmatic statesman who intellectually gathers that the elements of war are there in the real lives of the society while there is the existence of the circle of states. So, instead of dismissing the reality he tries for a system of theory so that the war ultimately causes less devastation to the stability of society and, instead, helps to march towards prosperity; and he defines towards an axiom "strength is of three kinds".

An analysis of the above description indicates that the root cause of war is an economic necessity. Kauṭilya accepts the proposition from the beginning that there is not a single state with which he is concerned, rather there are multiple of states about which he has to discuss in *Arthaśāstra*. The above description shows that he categorizes three types of states according to their economic and martial strengths *vis-à-vis* powerful, equally powerful and weaker. From this standpoint Kauṭilya considers that war is an intra-state reality and thus the art of war is a matter for the welfare of the state because the state defeated by another state suffers from the aggressors and the prosperities and virtues of the society suffer equally. So, for the protection of the state and the prosperity of the people the maintenance of the art of war is the duty of a wakeful king.

In this perspective it can be observed that *Arthaśāstra*

observes and stresses on the point that war is caused by an economic necessity.

The concept of war was essentially related to the concept of state in ancient India. Kauṭilya, followed to a certain extent, the previous writers on political science. The question of war was also dealt with in details in *Arthaśāstra* and as such, he referred to *kūṭa-yuddha* (treacherous war) and *prakāśa-yuddha* (open war). There is a *śloka* in *Arthaśāstra* that states:

> I (statehood or power of state) stay with the brave soldiers, industrialists, teachers and wise people. I install the patriots, the soldiers, scientists and men of medicine in the state.

Again, *R̥gveda* states:

> National language, own culture and devotion to motherland are the three elements which are essential for the well-being of people.

And, again Manu, the great law giver states:

> Since victory or defeat in war among contestant is seen to be impermanent, war shall be avoided.

In *Arthaśāstra*, we find that sixfold policy — peace, war, observance of neutrality, marching, alliance, and making peace with one contesting king and waging war with another — is considered by Kauṭilya as means by which the king tries to pass from the state of deterioration to that of stagnation, and from the latter to the state of progress. *Arthaśāstra* holds that when the country is full of born soldiers and possesses natural defensive positions such as mountains, forests, rivers and forts with only one entrance, it can easily repel the attack of its enemy and can harass the works of its enemy. Again, when the enemy suffers due to internal troubles and loss of energy or when the enemy is attacked by another country, the king can induce his (the enemy) subjects to immigrate into his country and then the king may increase his power and resources by keeping war or open hostility with such an enemy.

Here, Kauṭilya discusses how a king can prosper by war. So, war is regarded as a means of prosperity. War involves a desire — a desire for augmenting king's power and wealth.

Again, *Arthaśāstra* makes a distinction between *prakāśa yuddha* and *kūṭa-yuddha*. *Arthaśāstra* says:

> He (the king) who is possessed of a strong army, who has succeeded in his intrigues, and who has applied remedies against dangers may undertake an open fight, if he has secured a position favourable to himself; otherwise a treacherous fight.

According to Kauṭilya, *prakāśa yuddha* has a specific place and time and it is a fair or virtuous war. In case of a *prakāśa yuddha,* the king should call his army together and address them like this:

> I am a paid servant like yourselves; this country is to be enjoyed (by me) together with you; you have to strike the enemy specified by me.

According to *Arthaśāstra* though *prakāśa yuddha* is a fair or virtuous fight, it also involves some desire, a desire for enjoying the land.

Kauṭilya stresses on the point of the circle of states. The existence of multiple states side by side is one of the main causes of war. Whenever a state longs for its extension, it has to curb it out from another's land.

Arthaśāstra considers war mainly to be conducted by the warriors. He deals in details how the king should conduct his duties in respect of the multiple states, i.e. war, treaty, peace, forming a league with one state against another, selection of opportune and disfavoured periods, etc. He also stresses the "desire" element inherent to cause the war. The desire, here, is for the sovereignty — to maintain sovereignty by one weaker state with standing the onslaught of a more powerful one and, on the contrary, the desire of one powerful state to extend its sovereignty on another is also a cause for war.

Kauṭilya, while discussing about war, contributes two ideas which are embolded in the political history of states at a much later stage of the development of states in the process of history — the nationalist idea and the international law in the nascent stage. His arguments are involved from the question of sovereignty. A well-established sovereignty means the proper discharge by every man and community the work to which they are involved because if that is not done the strength of the state — intellectual, economic and martial — would be impaired. Hence, it is the duty of the king not to ravage on the people of the conquered state as they also form his subjects when his sovereignty is extended on them. So, Kauṭilya does not encourage indiscriminate pillage of the property of defeated nation though he permits that the wealth and properties of the defeated king may be confiscated by the victorious sovereign.

We have a definite idea of international consciousness in *Arthaśāstra*. Kauṭilya proposes to incite the "circle of states" or *maṇḍala* to preserve the balance of power against the over-rapid growth of a *madhyamā* king.

> If the *madhyamā* king is desirous of securing the friendship of the conqueror's would-be-friend, then having set his own and his friend's friends against the *madhyamā*, and having separated the *madhyamā* from the latter's friends, the conqueror should preserve his own friend; or the conqueror may incite the circle of states against the *madhyamā* by telling them: This *madhyamā* king, has grown haughty, and is aiming at our destruction; let us therefore combine and interrupt his march.

Here, Kauṭilya is very much traditional in nature. The concepts of *maṇḍala,* human laws of warfare, inter-state morality of a very high order are also expressed in other ancient Indian treatises like *Manu Saṁhitā, Rāmāyaṇa* and the *Mahābhārata.* So, Kauṭilya's assertions are not deviations from the Indian tradition.

2

Critical Analysis and Interpretation of War

Ancient Indian View

FROM our discussion in Chapter 1 it transpires that the ancient Indian authorities uphold a high standard of morality regarding the conduct of the combative warriors following the rules of war in general. War is thus considered differently than mere aggression in ancient India. Ancient thinkers hold the view that the purpose of war is the protection of the subjects and the establishment of sovereignty in a righteous way. War cannot be conducted for uncontrolled greed of power and wealth. It is obvious that *Māhābhārata, Manu Saṁhitā* and Arthaśāstra recommend war for the augmentation of power and wealth, but this power and wealth are for the development and prosperity of the state and not for the king himself. The real happiness of the king does not lie in mere power or money but in the happiness of his subjects. Ancient Indian authorities opine that through waging a war a king can attain *trivarga,* i.e. *dharma, artha* and *kāma* but there must prevail a balance between these three. The king would not be devoid of happiness. He can enjoy *dharma, artha* and *kāma* in a balanced way and these three are interdependent on each other. *Dharma* pervades both *kāma* and *artha* in the sense that one is to follow *kāma* and *artha* only under the guidance and regulation of *dharma*. If the king enjoys one of them excessively, then it hurts itself as well as the other two. It transpires that they argue for a balanced, enlightened approach for the king. According to the Indian tradition, *sāmyāvasthā* (position of equilibrium) of *trivarga* brought happiness.

Ancient Indian authors state that the king should restrain his sense-organs, i.e. he must regulate the demands of his lower being for the sake of the higher or the spiritual. In Upaniṣads, a distinction is made between *śreyaḥ* and *preyaḥ*, i.e. between the good and the pleasant. He who follows *śreyaḥ* attains the higher pursuits of life and one who follows *preyaḥ* fails in his aim. One should control his mere passions, gross desires (which are not desirable too) and his life should be regulated by higher faculties like reason, conscience, etc. According to Kauṭilya, a "saintly king" should first renounce the aggregate of the six enemies, i.e. when one abandons lust (*kāma*), greed (*lobha*), anger (*krodha*), vanity (*māna*), haughtiness (*mada*) and overjoy (*harṣa*), he can control his senses, and his success in study and discipline entirely depends on the restraint of sense-organs. Manu also suggests for the king the control of the senses, i.e. a king must be a *jitendriya* as such a king only can control his subjects properly. *Māhābhārata* also is of the opinion that a king should always have his senses under his control.

This control of the senses is very much essential for the equilibrium of *trivarga*, with his uncontrolled senses, passions and desires a king can ruin this equilibrium and consequently the happiness of his subjects. Individual morality and social morality are very much interdependent. Ancient Indian thinkers argue for good propensity in the self as well as in the social sphere. Good innate qualities in a balanced self lead to a balanced and prosperous society. With his uncontrolled senses and desires if the king ruins the equilibrium of *trivarga* then not only he leads his subjects to unhappiness but also ruins his own happiness because king's happiness rests on the welfare of the state and the people:

prajāsukhe sukham rājñaḥ, prajānām ca hite hitam |
nātmapriyam hitam rājñaḥ, prajānām tu priyam hitam ||

> In the happiness of his subjects lies his (king's) happiness; in their welfare his welfare; whatever pleases himself he shall not consider as good, but whatever pleases his subjects he shall consider as good. — *Arthaśāstra* of Kauṭilya, 1.19.5

The chief aims of an ideal king are the development, prosperity, protection and happiness of his subjects. The attainment of all these very much dependent on the attainment of *dharma, artha* and *kāma,* and for the attainment of *trivarga* war is necessary, ancient thinkers hold. But this war is not of the nature of aggression, they opine. Aggression necessarily involves uncontrolled desire, greed for power and wealth, feeling of anger and murderous intent, unlimited violence, i.e. uncontrolled senses which lead to the imbalance of *trivarga* and hence to the unhappiness of the subjects of the states involved in a war. Hence, a war conducted with aggressive attitude destroys the prime aims of a king — happiness and prosperity of his state. Rules of war and the post-war attitudes towards the conquered territory recommended by the ancient thinkers clearly show their preferences to the non-aggressive nature of the war. The principles of warfare and the attitude of the victor king in ancient India evidently indicate to the control of the senses of the fighting warriors which refers to the non-aggressive perspective of the war.

Trails of Contemporary Wars

The wars of contemporary world show quite different traits. Both the First and Second World wars, Vietnam War and the recent Afganistan and Iraq wars do not show regard to general civil rights or rules of general war laws towards the non-combatants or those who are not related actually in the conflict which is significantly emphasized by the ancient authorities when they laid down the principles of warfare. Very recently, sixteen Afghans including women and children were killed in their homes by a rogue US soldier in a pre-dawn rampage. An American soldier entered the homes of civilians in the southern Kandahar province and killed sixteen people including nine children and three women. Afghans have also faced numerous instances of civilian casualties from coalition military operations. American troops are still fighting in Afghanistan after ten years of conflict and the killing of Osama bin Laden. This incident recalls the infamous My Lai massacre in Vietnam in which a company of US soldiers slaughtered dozens of unarmed civilians. In Syria, bloodbath continues and the bodies of forty-seven women and children, some with their throats slit, were found in the restive Syrian city of Homs, causing hundreds of families fleeing the area. In Geneva, the UN refugee agency said 230,000 Syrians have fled their homes since the uprising against Assad's regime began last year. The UN says more than 7,500 people have been killed in the past twelve months. Last year, a special panel appointed by the UN Secretary-General Ban Ki-moon suggested that as many as 40,000 civilians died in the last few weeks of the bloody twenty-six-year civil war between the Sri Lankan government and the secessionist rebels of the Tamil Tigers, the LTTE. In all these contemporary cases the common people were subjected to murder and plunders. This shows the aggressive and immoral attitude of these wars, indeed. There are several common evils of modern/contemporary wars such as the wholesale disruption of civil life, non-utilization of cultivation, the destruction of buildings and cities, and works of art. All these evil consequences were at a minimum level or degree in the war as prescribed in the ancient Indian treatises.

Indian thinkers repeatedly recommend *dharma-yuddha* (just war) instead of *adharma-yuddha* (unjust war) for an ideal king. The concept of *dharma-yuddha* emerges from the situations where there are occasions in the life of nations when war becomes unavoidable; its avoidance leads to the sacrifice of all those that are worthwhile and as such it defeats the very purpose for which war is desired to be avoided. *Dharma-yuddha* is called for when all other means of reconciliation or endeavour to desist the enemies from the aggression are exhausted. So, *dharma-yuddha* is prescribed to be devoid of gross desires and it cannot be aggressive in nature. When one takes part in such a war he does so due to his sense of duty and nothing else. *Dharma-yuddha* is a "duty for duty's sake". It is the duty of a kṣatriya (king) to take part in a *dharma-yuddha* to protect the three elements — national language, own culture and devotion to motherland — which are essential for the well-being of his people.

Ancient treatises not only emphasize on the non-destructive righteous nature of the war, but the primordial elements of international consciousness are also traceable in the prescribed ethical nature of war. These treatises argue for some convention and rules for the treatment to be rendered to the soldiers and people of the vanquished enemies. The concepts of framing such rules originated from the conviction that senses needed to be tamed and controlled by the rational, humanistic spirit and vision. While war cannot be totally dismissed as uncalled for so long the states exist, the treatment to the enemies should be meted out also keeping the spirit in parity to the welfare of the society. Such laws are the conventional rules in the sphere of war devastations and it emanated from the quest for an ideal, just state.

Early Indian authorities considered war as the last resort, when other means, i.e. *sāma, dāna* and *bheda* failed; only then war was to be conducted. They were very much aware of the immediate devastating consequences of war. In Indian tradition some general duties (*sādhāraṇa dharma*) are prescribed which are to be followed by all irrespective of their *varṇa* (caste). This *dharma* includes *ahiṁsā, satya, akrodha, priya vacana, dayā, prema, svārtha tyāga, paranindā tyāga,* etc. Besides the observance of *rāja-dharma* which is a *viśeṣa dharma* of a king he also has to consider *sādhāraṇa dharma*s which are also conducive both to self-purification and maintenance of social order and welfare of the society. Conducting a war certainly violates *sādhāraṇa dharma*s like *ahiṁsā, akrodha,* etc. So, if the political objectives can be attained through *sāma, dāna* and *bheda,* i.e. avoiding the war, the king has to do that. But in spite of the evil consequences, at the failure of other means, Indian thinkers recommend war for the welfare of the state in the long run as it is the *rāja-dharma* of a king. But this war must be a *dharma-yuddha* and the recommended rules of war and post-war treatment towards the conquered people are quite compatible with the concept of *dharma-yuddha*. These precepts of war and the attitude of the victor king involve the elements of *sādhāraṇa dharma* like controlled desires, absence of unlimited greed for power and material wealth, avoidance of anger, murderous intent and unlimited violence, compassion and sympathy for the non-combatants or common people, etc. So, according to the Indian tradition, a king must observe a balance between *sādhāraṇa dharma* and *viśeṣa dharma* in the question of war with the prime objective of *lokasthiti* (maintenance of social order), *lokasiddhi* (preservation of social customs, etc.), *lokasaṁgraha* (social equilibrium), *lokakalyāṇa* (welfare of the society) and *lokayātrā* (social progress).

The Concept of Consequentialism

Ancient Indian concept of war is consequentialism, i.e. it believes that end justifies the means. Wars are held to be justified by what they achieve. For the prosperity and development of the state war is necessary though war is always considered as the last resort by the ancient authorities. In the case of *dharma-yuddha,* if war is not organized, society and state suffer. Their achievements are almost always bought at enormous cost, but sometimes, it may be said, the alternative to war is even more dire.

In the modern ethical thought the main moral objection against war is "war takes human life". Taking human life is objectionable because there is right to life, sanctity of life, utilitarian objections to killing and respect for autonomy.

According to the doctrine of the sanctity of human life, human being has some special value which is quite distinct from the value of the lives of other living beings. "Indicators of humanhood" includes self-awareness, self-control, a sense of the future, a sense of the past, the capacity to relate to others, concern for others, communication and curiosity. Human beings are rational and self-conscious beings. A theory of right to life holds that to have a right one must have the ability to desire that to which one has a right, so that to have a right to life one must be able to desire one's own continued existence.

Rules of warfare and post-war attitude prescribed in the ancient Indian treatises are quite compatible with the sanctity of life as well as the right to life. Post-war attitude repeatedly emphasizes on the protection of the common civilians. They are conscious and rational beings. Moreover, they are innocent human beings. So, their rationality, self-consciousness, free desire for their own continued existence should be treated with reverence and veneration. War certainly causes devastations, but the ancient authorities tried to minimize war casualties and devastations suffered by the common people through the rules of war and post-war attitude. Their right to life is not at all ignored. In the ancient Indian perspective king involves in a war not for his personal gain but for the welfare of his state. Well-being of the state necessarily means well-being of the subjects, i.e. welfare of the human beings. This ensures human and civil rights of the civilians which are the key concepts of the theory of the sanctity of human life and right to life.

The Concept of Utilitarianism

Utilitarianism judges actions by their tendency to maximize pleasure or happiness and minimize pain or unhappiness. The doctrine holds that a person, i.e. a self-conscious being has a conception of himself and he knows that he has a future. He also knows that his future existence could be cut short. If he thinks that this is likely to happen at any moment, his present existence will be fraught with anxiety, and will presumably be less enjoyable than if he does not think it is likely to happen for some time. If he learns that people like himself are very rarely killed, he will worry less. So, utilitarianism can defend a prohibition on killing persons on the ground that it will increase the happiness of people who would otherwise worry that they might be killed.

Ancient Indian thinkers are of the opinion that real happiness of the king lies in the happiness of his subjects. This is true even at the time of war. People of the conquered state naturally become the subjects of the victor ruler and hence, their happiness is the happiness of the victor king. If they (people of the conquered nation) fear that they may be killed at any moment then their present lives will be less happy and enjoyable. But as the victor king considers their happiness as his own so he tries to ensure this happiness and enjoyment like a father by providing protection, safety and security towards the conquered land and by the reconstruction of that state. The aim of the rules of war and the post-war attitude of the ancient India is to minimize pain and sufferings of the people of the states involved in war and to provide happiness and enjoyment for them.

Respect for autonomy is a basic moral principle. By "autonomy" is meant the capacity to choose, to make and act on one's own decisions. Rational and self-conscious beings presumably have this ability. Hence, killing a person who does not choose to die fails to respect that person's autonomy; and as the choice of living or dying is about the most fundamental choice anyone can make, the choice on which all other choices depend, killing a person who does not choose to die is the gravest possible violation of that person's autonomy.

Rules of war and post-war attitude, prescribed in the ancient Indian treatises, certainly recognize the free choice of living of the common people. Protection of the civilians, even of the conquered people is considered as a prime duty of the king involved in war. In the ancient Indian political treatises war-rules indicate that war should be taken place or occurred only between two armies and civilians should not be worsely affected in war. One should fight only with one person at a time. One who is on horseback should not run towards one who is seated on a chariot, one who is seated on a chariot can only rush towards another charioteer. Civilians or common people are not directly the parts of a war though their welfare is the chief aim of the king engaged in the war. As they are rational and self-conscious beings their autonomy or their choice of living cannot be ignored. The members of an army are also rational and self-conscious human beings, so they also have autonomy or the free choice of living. When a state is in war, army can not avoid of taking part in it. Naturally a question arises that whether their autonomy is violated when they are in war as the royal force of a state. It is true that the members of an army are human beings and they are also rational and self-conscious. So, they must have autonomy. But at the same time, army is a significant element of the state management and governance. Pragmatically, for the proper and accurate administration of the state and society war is quite inevitable and war without army or force is an absurd reality. War takes lives of the human beings (the members of an army), but for some greater noble cause, i.e. for the prosperity, security and development of the state and society this type of killing may be justified and moreover, rules of war in ancient India were quite sentient or conscious of minimizing the loss or damage of lives in war-ground. Hence, ancient authorities recognized the respect for autonomy in the case of royal army also and this is quite true from the perspectives of utilitarianism, doctrine of right to life and sanctity of life.

The actual conduct of the warriors in the battlefield might have differed from the ancient Indian war-ethics, but it is obvious that the ancient thinkers prescribed a high standard of moral political science on a very extravagant exercise associated with kingdom, state (of human society) in those early days pragmatically remaining conscious about social sciences.

3

Modern Indian Political Thought on War

THE ancient Indian view on the nature of war reveals its non-aggressive nature and considers war as the last resort. Naturally, one pertinent question creeps in here that whether modern and contemporary Indian political thought on war is quite analogous or something assorted/contrasting from the ancient views. The next discussion will be engaged in the search of the true significance of the concept of war as depicted in the modern and contemporary Indian political aspects; specially in the views of Mohandas Karamchand Gandhi, Sarvepalli Radhakrishnan, Sri Aurobindo and Vinayak Damodar Savarkar.

Mohandas Karamchand Gandhi (1869–1948)

M.K. Gandhi, in his political and social philosophy, always emphasizes his principle that mean should justify the end. If the end is attained by immoral and unfair means then it will not be of permanent nature. He is of the opinion that if one takes care of the means, the end will take care of itself. Violence is the means of war. As Gandhi is against any kind of violence, he is also against war. As the means of violence is not good, the end, i.e. war cannot be justified.

The British rule, a foreign power, occupied the system of administration or governance of India and the millions of Indians were oppressed and outraged by the British oppressors. Indian freedom struggle against this foreign administration may be considered or termed as war, for war means conflict between two powers. Here, the war is between two forces or powers — the British and the Indian people or the Indian nationalism. The actual armed conflict must be both intentional and widespread. Isolated clashes between rogue officers, or border patrols cannot be considered as wars. The onset of war requires a conscious commitment, and a significant mobilization, on the part of the belligerents in question. Indian freedom struggle has a conscious end and intention and it is also widespread. On this very basis Indian freedom movement may be termed as a war. A war is generally conceived as a military contest fought for political goals. Violence is used to bend or break the will of the adversary, but its targets and modes of application are generally determined by rules or norms. Indian freedom struggle has a definite political objective which is a significant feature of a war. Gandhi opined that those countries which were still suffering under feudal overlordship and colonial dependence should have the political freedom to determine their own future. With great psychological insight Gandhi warned the imperialistic countries that domination over others would jeopardize the moral fibre of the great powers. Hence, Gandhi approved and encouraged war in the form of national freedom struggle and he himself was a liberating force in the Indian War of Independence. According to Gandhi all war is unjust, but still the aspirant after freedom would distinguish between the aggressor and the defender, and render all moral support to the latter. Freedom struggle is a war to emancipate the exploited mankind from the injustice of the foreign oppressors, so this war may be approved though it should always be in the non-violent way. To attain justice, *swarāj*, i.e. the rule of all the people or the rule of justice is necessary and to have *swarāj* national freedom movement is required. This justice or freedom is political as well as economic. Gandhi knew that political freedom, devoid of its economic content, was a mere philosophical abstraction. Gandhi did not support the role of violence in the both forms of Indian War of Independence, i.e. freedom movement led by the Indian National Congress and the violent revolutionary movement. To him, non-violence was so significant that due to the violence in Chauri-Chaura near Gorakhpur of Uttar Pradesh he called off/suspended the non-coopertion movement. Gandhi was severely criticized for this but he justified his action on the ground that non-violence was the first article of his faith.

Gandhi interpreted the concept of courage in a very distinguishing and significant manner when he emphasized on the principle of non-violence. Courage, to him, is not concerned with violence. Non-violence or passive resistance needs tremendous courage and much more than in the violent means. According to him, India should win her freedom through non-violence and truth, and this victory will be permanent. But the victory attainable through violence is not permanent. Courage is the abandonment of the fear of death and this courage is not concerned with violence. Gandhi opines that "a nation which allows itself to be influenced by the fear of death cannot attain *swarāj*, and cannot retain it if somehow attained". Gandhi realized that non-violence required incredible faith and courage, which he realized not everyone possessed. He therefore advised that everyone need not keep to non-violence, especially if it were used as a cover for cowardice. He states:

> At every meeting I repeated the warning that unless they felt that in non-violence they had come into possession of a force infinitely superior to the one they had and in the use of which they were adept, they should have nothing to do with non-violence and resume the arms they possessed before. It must never be said of the *khudāī khidmatgārs* that

> once so brave, they had become or been made cowards under Badshah Khan's influence. Their bravery consisted not in being good marksmen but in defying death and being ever ready to bare their breasts to the bullets.
>
> — *Harijan,* 19 November 1938, p. 59

Gandhi commented the 1930s persecution of the Jews in Germany. He offered non-violence as a method of combating the difficulties Jews faced in Germany and stated that suffering voluntarily undergone would bring the Jews an inner strength and joy.

Ancient Indian political authorities considered righteous war as a means for the welfare and progress of the state. War involves violence, but they (ancient Indian thinkers) emphasized on the non-aggressive element of war to restraint this violence. Gandhi is an adherent of non-aggressive attitude of war though he is completely against of the violent means of war. In the ancient Indian view, war is for the development and progression of the state, in Gandhi's view also war, i.e. national freedom movement is for the liberation and emancipation of the people of the subservient state. Ancient Indian thought harmonized and brought into perfect agreement between violence and non-aggressive attitude of war; but in modern contemporary India, Gandhi recognizes non-violence as the only companion of the non-aggressive nature of war. As a believer in Jaina religion and philosophy Gandhi renounces all types of violence — physical, mental as well as verbal. Actions against the established authorities and actions carried out by, or ordered by the authorities— both are considered as "violence" to him if they are not in the peaceful means.

In a war, the conqueror acquires power; hence war and power are intimately related with each other. But Gandhi thinks that the real purpose of politics and power is social reform and the service to mankind and politics must involve religious aspects or religious values.

Gandhi tried to spiritualize politics and establish an intimate relation between religion and politics. To him, religion does not mean any religious dogmas or fundamentalism. Religion does not consist in worshipping god or reading a religious book. Religion involves all human activities. Religious life is identical with the concept of mankind. For him, religion is self-realization, suffering and sacrifices. Religion means the assertion of unity with god. It is a dynamic force. Hence, the incorporation of religion in politics meant a progressive movement towards justice and truth, for a man of religion will never tolerate any kind of oppression and exploitation. Gandhi states:

> To try to root out religion itself from society is a wild-goose chase. And where such an attempt to succeed, it would mean the destruction of society. — Varma 2006: 339

Here, Gandhi's view is quite similar to the ancient Indian view. Ancient Indian political thought denotes that the king must be powerful; without adequate and proper power and strength he cannot do good to his subjects. The ruler or the king may be involved in a war for attaining this power. Gandhi is also of the opinion that power contributes to the well-being and prosperity of the mankind and the power can be properly attained only by the means of truth and non-violence. Ancient Indian view on the other hand, approves violence as a means of war and consequently as a means for the acquisition of power and strength, though the traditional view also considers war or violence as the last resort which may be followed only after the failure of the principles of *sāma, dāna* and *bheda*. Here, Gandhi's view again reveals his non-aggressive attitude towards the concept of power and war.

Gandhi repeatedly states that in freedom struggle or war,

confidence and self-respect are required. People fighting for their national liberty should have self-respect for their past glory, culture and civilization.

The concept of *satyāgraha* of Gandhi means both truth (*satya*) and firmness (*āgraha*) involves force, "truth-force" or "soul-force" and this force resists injustice and evil though it is devoid of violence. *Satyāgraha* resists injustice, impure and evil as a moral force as opposed to brute and violent force. Hence to prevent or counteract injustice *satyāgraha* or non-violent force is quite adequate, the resistance of injustice does not need any violent force at all. One may resort to *satyāgraha,* wherever he wants to confront injustice — in the family or in the state. The war in the form of national independence struggle must be conducted by *satyāgraha,* i.e. in the pure non-violent way. After the 1930s during the various wars Gandhi opined that the Abyssinians, the Spaniards, the Chinese and the Poles could have prevented the aggressors in a non-violent means. Where justice prevails, truth and non-violence must incarnate; but in a society or a state where injustice is, e.g. in the British India, evil and injustice also should be opposed by truth and non-violence.

In Gandhi's view, state is an organization of violence; it is the organ of "violence in a concentrated and organized form". So it must be extinct. Gandhi is against any violent means followed by the state management and consequently he does not support the involvement of a state in a violent war as it hinders the development and progression of the state. He makes a distinction between the ideal society and *swarāj*. In the ideal society there will be no army; under *swarāj* army will function but in spite of the existence of the army the state must try to increase its perfection. With the increasing perfection, the state will proceed towards the non-violent goal. Gandhi visualized that in the future free India army will act only as a protective force and not for any aggression and offensive purpose.

To Gandhi, the proper and adequate means of war are non-violence and truth, i.e. *satyāgraha*. *Satyāgraha* is also a method or mode to remove injustice from the society and state, for war means actually war against evil and injustice. *Satyāgraha* is not for any personal gain, it is for the resistance of injustice and for the formation of a morally strong society and state. Here, Gandhi's view is similar to the ancient Indian concept of war that war is for the betterment of the state and society though their approaches are different.

Gandhi condemns violence on moral grounds and he accepts the absolutism of *ahiṁsā* (non-violence). He believes that violence interrupts the real revolution of the social structure. *Satyāgraha* can revolutionize social ideals. He states:

> The science of war leads one to dictatorship, pure and simple. The science of non-violence alone can lead one to pure democracy. Power based on love is thousand times more effective and permanent than power derived from fear of punishment. . . . It is a blasphemy to say non-violence can be practised only by individuals and never by nations which are composed of individuals . . . the nearest approach to purest anarchy would be a democracy based on non-violence. . . . A society organized and run on the basis of complete non-violence would be the purest anarchy.
>
> If the non-violent society is attacked from without, there are two ways open to non-violence. To yield possession, but non-cooperate with the aggressor . . . prefer death to submission. The second way would be non-violent resistance by the people who have been trained in the non-violent way. The unexpected spectacle of endless rows upon rows of men and women simply dying rather than surrender to the will of an aggressor must ultimately melt him and his soldiers. . . . A nation or group which has made non-violence its final policy cannot be subjected to slavery even by the atomic bomb. . . . The level of non-violence in that nation, if

> that even happily comes to pass, will naturally have risen so high as to command universal respect.[1]

Gandhiji commented upon the 1930s persecution of the Jews in Germany within the context of *satyāgraha*. In the November 1938 article, on the Nazi persecution of the Jews, he offered non-violence as a solution.

> The German persecution of the Jews seems to have no parallel in history. If there ever could be a justifiable war in the name of and for humanity, a war against Germany, to prevent the Wanton persecution of a whole race, would be completely justified. But I do not believe in any war. A discussion of the pros and cons of such a war is therefore outside my horizon or province.[2]

Although Gandhi repeatedly emphasizes on the principle of non-violence, he also opines that sometimes violence is permissible. When one is confronted with a choice between violence and cowardice, violence is more preferable. In his view, "cowardice itself is violence of a subtle and therefore dangerous type and far more difficult to eradicate than the habit of physical violence. A coward never risks his life." A question naturally comes in our mind that when a state is facing foreign aggression what will be the role of that state or country in the opinion of Gandhi. If that aggression cannot be obstructed or resisted by non-violence and truth, then violence will not be wrong in this case, he holds. Violence is more preferable than to surrender national culture, language and freedom to a foreign power in a cowardly manner. This view resembles to the non-aggressive traditional Indian view that war or violence is the last resort, only after the failure of *sāma*,

---

1 M.K. Gandhi, *For Pacifists*, ed. Bharatan Kumarappa, Ahmedabad: Navajivan Publishing House, 1949.

2 M.K. Gandhi, "A New Violent Look at Conflict and Violence", in *Harijan*, 26 November 1938.

dāna and *bheda* principles violent means to be applied.

In war against the British power, Gandhi followed the principle of *satyāgraha*. *Satyāgraha* can be resorted through non-cooperation, which is a method for the demonstration of the protest of the people against the injustice of the foreign rule. Non-cooperation of the people is a non-aggressive war method of Gandhi, which installs courage and fearlessness in the people.

Passionate or peevish nationalism sometimes leads to war. Nationalism, which desperately attempts to establish its own superiority, sometimes occupies other nations through aggressive war. It also gives rise to the internal war within the country. In Nazi Germany drastic and reckless nationalism of Hitler generated an internal war between the Germans and the Jews. Gandhi was against of this type of national sentiment which contained antagonistic and assertive elements within it.

Gandhi stresses on the non-exploitative attitude towards the other nations. He expects that independent India will never exploit other states of the world. India will recognize equal rights of all other nations and endeavour to establish international harmony. In his words, "through the deliverance of India, I seek to deliver the so-called weaker races of the earth from the crushing heels of Western exploitation in which England is the greatest partner." Here, non-aggressive concept of international harmony and international consciousness is traced in Gandhi's voice.

Gandhi's view delineates that one nation should not be subordinated by another. He opines that death is more preferable than bondage both in the cases of individual and nation. This non-aggressive outlook of Gandhi clearly opposes any violent war between two nations or the possession and subjugation of one country by another through offensive means.

Gandhi is of the view that nationalism is good but if this nationalism involves narrowness and selfish spirit then it leads us to evil consequences. In *Young India* he remarks:

> It is not nationalism that is evil, it is the narrowness, selfishness, exclusiveness which is the leave of modern nations, that is evil. — *Young India,* 18 Jun 1925, p. 211

Gandhi expects that people will contemplate on the well-being of the entire human race and will not be confined to the narrow cordon or limitation of their own nationalism. In his view that world will be ideal which is based on peace and mutual co-operation and an international organization, consists of the representatives of the various nations or states having faith or confidence in the principle of non-violence, will be there. This organization will recognize and endeavour for the preservation of the equality and liberty of the mankind and to actualize this purpose it will try to remove imperialism, communalism, war and racial antagonism. Isolated independence for Gandhi is not the ultimate goal of world-states; the better mind of the world rather desires not the absolutely independent states conflicting with each other, but a federation of friendly independent states. The concept of the international consciousness of Gandhi indicates that he is against the aggressive offensive notion of war.

Gandhi's non-violence is the first article of his faith and it is also the last article of his creed. But there are some controversial cases where apparently it appears that Gandhi supports violent methods to some extent.

In 1906, after the British introduced a new poll-tax, Zulus in South Africa killed two British officers. In response, the British declared war against the Zulus. Gandhi actively encouraged the British to recruit Indians. He argued that Indians should support the war efforts in order to legitimize their claims to full citizenship. The British, however, refused to commission Indians as army officers. None the less, they accepted Gandhi's offer to let a detachment of Indians volunteer as a stretcher-bearer corps to treat wounded British soldiers. This corps was commanded by Gandhi. Gandhi urged the Indian population in South Africa to join the war through his columns in *Indian Opinion*:

> If the government only realized what reserve force is being wasted, they would make use of it and give Indians the opportunity of a through training for actual warfare.

In April 1918, during the latter part of First World War, the Viceroy invited Gandhi to a war conference in Delhi. Perhaps to show his support for the Empire and help his case for India's independence, Gandhi agreed to actively recruit Indians for the war effort. In a June 1918 leaflet entitled "Appeal for Enlistment", Gandhi wrote:

> To bring about such a state of things we should have the ability to defend ourselves, that is, the ability to bear arms and to use them. . . . If we want to learn the use of arms with the greatest possible dispatch, it is our duty to enlist ourselves in the army.

He did however stipulate in a letter to the Viceroy's private secretary that he "personally will not kill or injure anybody, friend or foe". Gandhi's war recruitment campaign brought into question his consistency on non-violence as his friend Charlie Andrews confirms:

> Personally I have never been able to reconcile this with his own conduct in other respects, and it is one of the points where I have found myself in painful disagreement.[3]

Gandhi's private secretary also acknowledges that:

---

[3] C.F. Andrews, *Mahatma Gandhi's Ideas*, Macmillan, 1930, p. 133.

> The question of the consistency between his creed of *ahiṁsā* (non-violence) and his recruiting campaign was raised not only then but has been discussed ever since.[4]

Again, Gandhi supported the British power in Second World War, which broke out in 1939 when Nazi Germany invaded Poland. Initially Gandhi favoured offering "non-violent moral support" to the British effort, but other Congress leaders were offended by the unilateral inclusion of India in the war, without consultation of the people's representatives. All leaders resigned from office. After long deliberations, Gandhi declared that India could not be party to a war ostensibly being fought for democratic freedom, while that freedom was denied to India itself.

All these exceptional cases certainly raise the question regarding Gandhi's consistent faith in non-violence. But in spite of these exceptions, his philosophy and life-long political activities clearly reveal his non-aggressive attitude of war which is based on his firm conviction on the principle of non-violence. His methodology has a pragmatic and an idealist aspect while his philosophy is purely idealistic. His sense of realism leads him to lend his occasional support for these exceptional cases, though he knows that these are far from perfect. Gandhi's concept is compatible and analogous to Pacifism which holds the view that moral concepts can certainly be applied fruitfully to international affairs. There is always some better resolution to the problem than fighting. Exceptional cases were some special, practical, political and social situations, which demanded those reversions or deviations.

Sarvepalli Radhakrishnan (1888–1975)

In this discourse, war concept of Sarvepalli Radhakrishnan is

---

4 Mahadev Desai, *Day-to-Day with Gandhi*, Secretary's Diary, vol. 1, 1930.

mainly based on his work *Is This Peace*?. In this book he analyses and demonstrates war-time and post-war circumstances of the two world wars and interprets the nature of war and peace condition of the modern world.

War, Radhakrishnan thinks, corrupts many things and one of the many casualties of war is intellectual honesty. Though in the modern world people have adequate knowledge and power to generate wealth, protect or sustain life and promote human welfare, they are using this knowledge and power for death and annihilation, i.e. for war. Hence, war situation is against of the creation of wealth, preservation of life and human welfare.

After the First World War, political authorities of the leading nations committed that in the new world human liberty and national security would not be the mere slogans but the pragmatic realities. But Second World War betrayed that hope of establishing freedom and security which reflects that war situation is not at all a patron for human liberty and safety, and security of a nation.

Radhakrishnan expresses the view that in the modern, contemporary world, war has become totally mechanical, inhuman and unendurable in nature and man is the worst enemy of his own species when he involves in such a war. Rational and sensible individual must protest against this war. So, Radhakrishnan criticizes and condemns inhuman and automated war policy which is contrary to the laws of god and humanity.

In his book *Is This Peace*?, Radhakrishnan quotes President Truman and supports his view. President Truman, welcoming the delegates to the United Nations Conference at San Franscisco, said:

> With ever-increasing brutality and destruction, modern warfare, if unchanged, would ultimately crush all

> civilization. We still have a chance — between the alternatives of the continuation of the international chaos or the establishment of a world organization for the enforcement of peace.[5]

Radhakrishnan approves the opinion of President Truman that uncontrolled atrocities and devastation of the modern war are a severe threat to the human civilization. War which involves the principles of destruction, annihilation and brutality is standing in the way of human progression and civilization. If the end of a war does not assure the establishment of humanity and liberty, liberty from physical danger and perpetual anxiety then that war should be opposed. Radhakrishnan is of the opinion that modern war is against of humanity, liberty, physical and mental peace.

At the end of Second World War, defeated nations — Germany and Japan — were not included as the members of the United Nations. Radhakrishnan severely opposed this view and opined that nations with immense potential resources like Germany and Japan should not be out of United Nations only due to thoughts of revenge and resentment. Defeated people are also human beings. Naturally they possess ambitions and vanities like the other nations. So, they should not be treated more criminal than others. Here, non-aggressive humanistic attitude towards the defeated or conquered powers is evident. In this regard, Radhakrishnan supported the view of Marshal Stalin that Hitler should not be identified with the German people or the German state.

Radhakrishnan severely criticized the deliberate, calculated and cynically executed massacre of the innocent Jews in the Nazi Germany. But simultaneously, he is also against of the attitude of the victor powers towards defeated Germany after

---

[5] S. Radhakrishnan, *Is This Peace*? Bombay: Hind Kitabs, 1945, pp. 4-5.

the First World War, he condemns specially the economic exploitation of the Germany by the victor nations and due to this injustice Germany became so arrogant. The conqueror did not have any sympathy or generosity for the defeated Germany. Radhakrishnan expresses the view that injustice and inhumane attitude towards Germany from the victor parties for the twenty years gave rise to the arrogant or boastful war effort of Germany. War actually means war against injustice, the aim of war is to resist injustice. Here, the view of Radhakrishnan is quite compatible with the traditional Indian concept. He repeatedly emphasizes on the traditional ancient post-war attitude of affinity and concern towards the defeated, powerless, vanquished nations.

Japan was an ally of Britain and France in the First World War. As a consequence of this, when Japan invaded Manchuria and Korea, attacked China and occupied some area neither Britain nor France, i.e. no big powers of the world, condemned and opposed this aggressive attitude of Japan which was contrary to the International Law. This view of Radhakrishnan delineates international consciousness which considers that aggression is inconsistent with the international peace and harmony. Again, Western democratic powers did not oppose the aggression of Germany, Italy and Japan and they remained completely indifferent as the mere observers until Poland was attacked by Germany. They were apathetic towards the losses and sufferings of the countries due to this antagonistic and assertive approach of Italy, Japan and Germany. Radhakrishnan criticizes this narrow nationalism of the European big powers which prevented them to oppose the aggression; this constricted and selfish nationalism did not show any respect towards the international laws and harmony and created another world war.

Radhakrishnan denounces and criticizes the implementation of the "flying bomb" by Germany and also the use of atomic power by the Allied Nations for all these were against the principle of humanity. Again, his view is here non-aggressive and humanistic. In this war (Second World War), no poison gas was used, not from any ethical considerations but from the fear of reprisal; every nation knew that the opponent state also possessed poison gas and they might apply it. But in the case of atomic bomb, as Axis power did not have it, Allied Nations quite comfortably used it without any fear of retaliation. Here, Radhakrishnan portrays a pragmatic empirical aspect of war — war method or war principle should be adopted after a clear and distinct observation and analysis of the capability and power of the enemy states. Moreover, he makes a distinction between war and massacre. Attack on the unarmed civilians is not war, but simply killing which is completely immoral. So, he stresses on the implementation of the humanistic rules in war.

The allied powers justify the use of the atomic bomb on the ground that it shortened the duration of the war. Radhakrishnan opines that this cannot be a justification for the application of such a weapon which is completely antagonistic to humanity. Nations engaged in war consider the enemy states as the demon or evil spirits and try to treat them in a brutal and cruel manner. But this should not be the attitude of the civilized world, Radhakrishnan holds and once again he supports the humanistic attitude towards the opponent states. He closely observes that, allied powers are not severely condemned or blamed for the use of the atomic power though it clearly violates international law and morality and the sole justification for its use can be nothing other than the military necessity. Here, Radhakrishnan expresses a very pragmatic view, recognizes the significant role of the morality in war and expresses respect or reverence towards the international law and principle. He delineates that even the military necessity cannot be a satisfactory and adequate ground for the practical use of inhuman weapon like atomic bomb.

While discussing the decision of the War Crimes Commission after the Second World War, Radhakrishnan agrees with the Commission that demolition of the cities and civilians (e.g. Hiroshima and Nagasaki) is a serious war crime. Again, the use of any dreadful and barbaric weapon or war method cannot be justified or defended on the basis of military necessity. Hence, he repeatedly condemns the aggressive element of war, stresses on the humanistic aspect and opines that no unethical warlike skill or military tactics is right for the attainment of victory. War should be fair fight and should be devoid of mass murder. To avoid injustice, a self-examination is required before disbursing justice or retribution. Here, Radhakrishnan states about moral and fair post-war attitude towards the war criminals and holds the view that war itself is a crime which is the concentration of all crimes. War may be started with a noble purpose — to fight the evil, brute force, injustice and exploitation; but if that war ultimately goes against the human and civilized values then its magnanimous purpose cannot defend it. In this case, Radhakrishnan explains and evaluates war situation from a very practical and empirical point of view, and he makes a pragmatic observation that a war, started with a glorious and virtuous cause, generally ends with an inhuman and uncivilized feature which cannot be approved or encouraged.

Radhakrishnan contemplates that the allied powers became conquerer in the Second World War not for their love of freedom or morality, but for their physical power, developed scientific techniques, stable economy, strong determination to defeat the opponent without any touch or feeling of conscience, honour and international morality. Moreover, technological backwardness of the Axis power carried victory for the allied group. This victory is not so glorious, Radhakrishnan makes a remark, as it completely lacks compunction/conscience and fairness. So, magnificent and distinguished conquest should contain strong and assertive ethical element. Again, he makes a practical observation that scientific and technological advancement is an eloquent means by which victory can be achieved in the modern warfare.

Radhakrishnan is of the opinion that defeated powers should be treated with tolerance, sympathy, goodwill, faith and understanding, and this can build a better world. We should try to establish good international relation and co-operation among nations even with the defeated states and try to prevent aggressive wars. Conquerors should have a goodwill for providing economic and political securities to the vanquished nations. Narrow nationalism inspires a state to think about its own security alone and the Second World War is an evil consequence of the post-First World War confined nationalism and revengeful attitude of the victor powers. Hence, Radhakrishnan is against the narrow, closed and constricted nationalism and retributive treatment towards the defeated ones. Narrow nationalism and vindictive conduct give rise to the unpleasant evil consequence of war and this assertion proclaims his piercing moral international consciousness.

Contemplating on the modern and contemporary world, Radhakrishnan comments that in the world of atomic bombs every nation has to possess atomic power if it wants to remain sovereign and independent. But this atomic power, if uncontrolled, ultimately will destroy the human race. Radhakrishnan is quite aware of the practical evil outcome or consequence of the modern world war perspective and states that in the atomic age sovereignty and freedom of a nation depend on the possession of the atomic power which is terrific and alarming for the existence of the mankind.

Radhakrishnan imparts/reveals his view that narrow or closed nationalism should be abandoned/cast off/given up.

One cannot be a true patriot without humanity. Nations should consider the interest of the entire world besides their own national spirits and he recommends for an international organization which will administer the world peace. This advocacy indicates to his international awareness.

In the Security Council of the United Nations, formed after the Second World War, representatives were selected on the basis of power. Radhakrishnan raises the question regarding the true nature of the power, i.e. what is the power concept of the modern world? He elucidates that it is difficult to define this power. If territorial extent, strategical situation, self-sufficiency in resources, agricultural and industrial prosperity, fertility of the land, abundant mineral resources are considered as the criteria/touchstones of the power then India should be regarded as one of the great powers of the world which is quite capable of controlling the world peace. But the selection of the representatives in the Security Council indicates to a very divergent and unusual power concept of the modern world. These members of the Security Council are not so engrossed and enthusiastic in the establishment of the world peace.

Radhakrishnan closely observes that the structure of the United Nations is such that it can oppose the aggression of the small powers but not of the big powers. This power of resistance associated with the power concept of the modern world. If this power concept is accurate, fair and ethical then there will be no aggression, for powerful states will have a sympathy and consideration for the rights of the less powerful nations. But this is not the real picture and so antagonistic attitude exists. Radhakrishnan notices that in the modern contemporary world aggression is related with the imperfect power notion.

He makes an assessment that tension and hatred among

different nations generate aggression and the international organization like the United Nations can prevent this aggression by resolving all these tensions and disputes. Aggression is adverse to the international law and peace and so it must be restrained and thwarted for the initiating confirmation of the world peace.

It is the view of Radhakrishnan that the big powers should be self-restrained for the maintenance of world peace. If there is no self-restraint, i.e. no control of the passions and desires then each and every nation wants to be more powerful and it will attack other countries. Aggression and war will be the inevitable consequences of such unrestricted desires and passions. Hence, to prevent aggression and war nations must have control over their desires of being more powerful. In this case, his observation is quite similar to the ancient Indian view that uncontrolled passion is a principal cause of war and aggression.

Radhakrishnan opines from a practical perspective that the feeling of danger brought the great powers together and when this feeling disappeared they started to separate themselves. So, their co-operation aimed only at the protection of their own interests and not at the maintenance of the world peace.

The ancient Indian political treatises like *Mahābhārata* show the evidence that different states usually were united for the war. But in those days that union or unity was not only for the interest of the nations but also for the preservation of *dharma* or the conservation of the society, i.e. for the prevention of injustice and evil. On the other hand, in the modern world, he observes that the unification of the big powers is only for the interest of their own and so, it transpires that there is a colossal contrast between the ancient Indian and the modern contemporary ethical perspectives.

At the end of the Second World War, the decision was taken for the internationalization of the main industrial belt of Germany, i.e. Rhineland, because due to this control of German industry, Germany would never again be a danger. Therefore, it is assumed that an economically powerful state may be aggressive and may be involved in war against other countries and economic power is a source for aggressive attitude. Here, Radhakrishnan's observation is quite different from the ancient Indian political view. Ancient view is of the opinion that a king involves in a war to make his state prosperous for prosperity and resources are required for the progression of the state. But modern contemporary world believes that an immensely economically powerful state may have aggressive attitude and it will be a danger for the security of the other nations. Ancient view holds that for its own development, i.e. for a national cause or nationalism a state must be economically powerful. If required, for this national cause, a state may attack other states and involve in a war though war is always considered as the last resort. But in the present-day world an economically powerful state is not satisfied only with its own prosperity and development, i.e. not only with its own national cause or nationalism; rather it aspires to be more and more powerful and it involves in an aggressive war. So, a resourceful nation attacks other nations due to its uncontrolled passions and desires which indicate that for the maintenance of the world peace and to suppress the aggression, passions and desires must be restrained.

As a post-war policy concerning the maintenance of the world peace great powers of the world strived after the possession over the strategically significant places and America, Britain and the other big powers were not interested in the proposal of independence for colonial peoples as they thought that it would be an obstruction to the world peace. Moreover they craved for the possession of a industrial and economic power which they believe, is necessary for world peace. So, contemporary world conceives that in the interest of the world peace economic power, military bases, colonial power, i.e. control of the other nations are inevitable. It means that world peace is conditioned by the supremacy of the big powers over the small ones and if the colonial independence, i.e. the freedom of the all countries of the world is acknowledged or promised, world peace will not be ascertained. Radhakrishnan considers this principle of the great powers as only another name for military imperialism. Empirically, in this way, peace cannot be long-lived as the subjugated colonial countries naturally fight for their independence.

The peace concept of the present contemporary world is a concept of imperialism. It refers to the possession over the weak and small nations by the big ones and freedom and independent existence of all the countries of the world is not compatible with the world peace. Again, even the big powers quarrel with each other in the question of colonial possession and it transpires that though apparently colonial possession is justified on the ground of enduring world peace but actually this possession is only for the self-interest of a nation. The interests of the great powers are quite contradictory to each other and hence conflict is destined and inescapable. Colonial possession is adversary to the human value and human dignity. No individual can be deprived of the liberty and basic needs for his race or colour. Human values, human dignity and freedom are the preliminary conditions for the world peace and so all these should be protected. Apart from the material causes and uncontrolled passions, violation of human values and dignity certainly generate war situation. For the suppression of clashes and rivalries and for the world peace, Radhakrishnan suggests that the international organization should treat all the countries as equal, states must be confident as their lack of confidence causes arm race, states must be devoid of narrow nationalism and should have courageous statesmanship which will ensure the liberty and happiness of the common people of all lands.

While stressing on the world peace, he is also aware of the fact that war is a practical reality as there is the existence of many states and so war cannot be absolutely obliterated. But aggressive war should be prevented and the antagonistic element has to be minimized. For this, an international organization, approved by the entire world, is to be established which will have the authority to declare war only against aggressive nations and it is not any individual country that will declare war but the international authority.

Radhakrishnan makes an assessment that treaties, settlements, alliances are not adequate for permanent peace, for they are concerned only with the existing causes of war and not with the real causes. Competitive ways of life of the present-day society, national and class division, racial and religious aspects are the real causes of conflict. Mere treaties and settlements cannot alter all these; persistence of these facts confirms conflicts and clashes and hence war is a practical reality. War cannot be totally wiped out or eliminated but it must be non-aggressive as far as possible.

He observes and recommends the fullest development of human personality, defence of human liberty against the encroachments by the state, inalienable right of all nations to freedom and equality to other nations, rejection of violence and falsehood as instruments of either domestic or international policy as the means for minimizing war. Hence, his humanistic view stresses on the human liberty, dignity and equality for the avoidance of clashes. There may be some apparent causes of conflict, but actually violation of liberty, etc. give rise to the war.

If war or war in the form of freedom struggle for the attainment of liberty becomes inevitable then also conscience of humanity or morality should not be left behind, argues Radhakrishnan. The ethical perspective of war is significant and politics is a branch of ethics. The consideration of the ethical aspect of war as the cardinal issue may create a control over the aggressive element of war which is required for the enduring world peace. The existence of many states makes war and conflict a pragmatic and empirical reality. In the contemporary world, science has made nations dependent on each other for their means of living, but in spite of this dependence there are conflicts of interests among these nations and it proves that not only the economic consideration but also the cultural co-operation, exchange of cultural view are called for the establishment of world peace.

In his article "Mahatma Gandhi" Radhakrishnan comments that government and power are responsible for the modern war and not the common mass. The ruling class appeals to the fear, self-interest and pride of the common people and seduce them from their humanity.

In *East and West in Religion,* Radhakrishnan states that our symbols, trade, property, empire, tradition and all the unconscious influences of education glorify the concept of the independent sovereign state and the suppression of other nations as a symbol of loyalty to one's own state. He is against of this type of narrow and confined nationalism which is a significant cause of war.

Radhakrishnan indicates in his *Religion and Society* that, in the ancient Indian ideal political thought, non-violence was considered as the highest duty though it had some exceptions. He makes a practical observation that the existing societies are not ideal, but the deviations from it. So, war is a practical reality. *Ahiṁsā* is the highest goal, but in the practical world violence is prevalent and we have to accept it as a practical fact. The source of aggression is power or force of a state. When a state possesses advantageous numbers, strategic position, control of raw materials, developed agriculture, industry and arms it becomes more powerful than the others and then it tries to conquer and control the other nations which leads to an aggressive conflict. This power or force should be devoid of greed and it must be related to humanity. A state must be powerful for its prosperity and national interest; but this power should be ethical, human and non-aggressive. Otherwise, other weaker states of the world will suffer from its aggression. So, power itself is not an evil matter, power which is unethical and greedy is the source of aggression. Power which considers race more important than the individual is the source of aggression and antagonism. Aggressive war and uncontrolled power are not good for human progression and civilization; rather, civilizations based on endurance, understanding, tolerance, etc. are long-lived.

Radhakrishnan's view on war is quite compatible with the Indian tradition. The existence of war is a fact, but its aggressive element has to be reduced. War must have a moral aspect. Loss of lives and loss of property are the practical consequences of war; in spite of all these war should contain humanistic elements. States involved in a war have to realize the significance of humanistic element, human dignity and values which may contribute to the curtailment and deceleration of aggressive attitude and losses. Non-violence, as an ideal is no doubt praiseworthy, but violence is a reality in this world. So, war is. We must have an endeavour to make it non-aggressive.

Sri Aurobindo Ghosh (1872–1950)

Sri Aurobindo Ghosh from his very early life had a clear conception of the British government. He firmly believed that

British government must be driven out from India and he stressed on the armed rebellion or war in the form of freedom struggle. Aurobindo suggested the Congress to adopt the policy of "blood and fire" for the nationalist movement instead of prayers and petitions. His role was of an extremist leader, he wrote some revolutionary writings and he organized the youth for an armed rebellion. So, Aurobindo was in favour of the armed rebellion or war for the nationalist struggle.

For Aurobindo, nationalism is not a mere political concept; it is a religion. Nation is the divine mother. It has to be adored with devotion and sacrifice. But his concept of nationalism is not narrow, it is broader and comprehensive than mere patriotism. For this divine, ethical nationalism he supported armed rebellion. So, according to Aurobindo war in the form of freedom struggle requires violence, the concept of nationalism or national spirit though this nationalism is not selfish or confined in nature. He holds the view that nationalism is based on religion or spiritualism, so it is permanent and universal. This is a unique concept of nationalism.

Aurobindo conceives that political independence is essential for the progression and development of the state. Development of the nation depends on the political independence and this political independence can be attained through violent freedom struggle and not by the prayers and petitions to the British. His concept of nationalism is not aggressive, narrow or fanatic. Aurobindo expresses the view that instead of becoming a master India will contribute to the development, unity and equality of the mankind by her spiritual and ethical approach.

He believed that complete independence is the goal of our national struggle and that freedom is essential for the progression of humanity. His concept of international consciousness is expressed here. He wished for the liberty of his own country, i.e. of Mother India but at the same time he offered hopes or felt encouraged that this freedom will serve the entire mankind.

Aurobindo firmly believes in *Bhagavad-Gītā* and holds the view that if required, implementation of violence is permissible for getting freedom. If the glorious end of the national freedom movement cannot be achieved by other means then violence shall be followed. He repeatedly stresses that force or violence should be implemented when it is absolutely necessary in a quite favourable time.

His stand against the concept of imperialism and colonialism is firm. A perfect society, he holds, should contain the features of equality and brotherhood. When a nation attains liberty, it should work for the welfare of the entire mankind instead of patronizing narrow, confined nationalism. True and real nationalism is an approbation for the establishment of the international fraternity. His international consciousness is a corollary of his philosophical perception that the entire human generation is the creation of God, we all are the parts of God and hence we are related to each other.

Aurobindo believes that nationalism is a spell or development for the establishment of true internationalism. Every nation should be free and equal. World union should be based on the spiritual unification and not on the mere diplomacy or coercion. He has a firm conviction that freedom of the nation is essential and for that freedom violence may be the means, if required. But that national struggle or nationalism should not be aggressive for nationalism is the preliminary stage for the establishment of world union or internationalism. National liberty and identity should not be forsaken, rather through the national identity world union may be constituted.

Complete and comprehensive independence requires

intensive nationalism and for the achievement of this freedom Aurobindo encourages/reinforces militant nationalism. Without complete independence, no real development is possible in India. Political freedom is prerequisite/essential for the social, educational, industrial as well as moral development of the nation.

Aurobindo's concept of nationalism is purely spiritual and religious, and not of aggressive nature. India is not merely a geographical entity, but she has spiritual and religious perspectives. He conceives India as the divine mother who always demands sacrifice of her sons and nationalist freedom struggle is a religious, moral and spiritual movement. Nationalism signifies the identification of an individual with Mother India.

Aurobindo believes that nationalism in the true sense is not at all contrary to the concept of internationalism and human unity. World union will be constituted by the free, equal nations who will not try to subjugate the one another. Every nation must possess the national essence and spirit as well as the international consciousness and they should be prepared for the subordination of their interests to the interest of the mankind.

Aurobindo emphasizes not only on the external political freedom but also on the inner spiritual liberty, i.e. freedom from want and material insecurity. This freedom from the gross desires, wants and materialism makes his concept of political freedom and nationalism non-aggressive. Antagonistic and aggressive attitude involves gross desires and greed for power and wealth. Suppression of these material instincts moderates or tone down antagonistic feelings.

In Aurobindo's view nationalism is our identification with Mother India. She is our mother, we are her children. For her economic, social, educational, moral developments and progress we certainly have complete political independence, in absence of which these developments are not possible because absolute independence is a prerequisite for the enjoyment of our lives according to our own culture and ideals. Aurobindo suggests violent methods for the national freedom movement as in his philosophy "means" are not so significant, the "end" is crucial and that end is the political liberation. Mother India is chained and her political–cultural heritage and essence are strangulated by the foreign power. An individual usually tries to take resort to any means to save his life, similarly the Indian people may also adopt any means to attain political independence.

Aurobindo suggests war in the form of national liberation movement, which may be organized in violent process against the British oppressors who snatches and grabs our political independence. Means are not so important and resistance of violence by violence is quite justified. In his book *The Doctrine of Passive Resistance* Aurobindo (2002: 29-31) says:

> Liberty is the life-breath of a nation; and when the life is attacked, when it is sought to suppress all chance of breaking by violent pressure, any and every means of self-preservation becomes right and justifiable — just as it is lawful for a man who is strangled to rid himself of the pressure on his throat by any means in his power. It is the nature of the pressure which determines the nature of resistance, where, as in Russia the denial of liberty is enforced by legalized murder and outrage, or as in Ireland formerly by brutal coercion, the answer of violence to violence is justified and inevitable.

He holds the view that violent national struggle may be conducted in two ways — organized armed revolt and terrorism. With a realistic and empirical analysis he observes that British military power is not so immensely powerful that it could not be encountered. India does not have sufficient arms for the revolt, so he suggests that India may bring arms from outside. Moreover, as the part of the freedom movement Aurobindo proposes guerilla warfare and a general revolt in the Indian army. He supports terrorism as a means of attaining liberty, though he expresses his pragmatic view that it is not so realistic to expect random act of assassination. Aurobindo prefers the organized armed revolt to the terrorist activities.

Inhuman, ruthless, unsympathetic oppression of the British government for a long period and the lamentable/regrettable failure of the moderate policy (prayers, petitions, etc.) awakened/reminded Aurobindo to believe that for political freedom violence was inevitable. On the basis of the analysis of the then Indian social and political conditions Aurobindo adopted this practical view/decision.

Aurobindo's view or idea was charged after the partition of Bengal in 1905 and he then supported passive resistance as a method of freedom struggle. The aim of the passive resistance was to make the foreign administration ineffective by refusing to do anything which might help the administration. But he also made it clear that passive resistance might turn to be violent in case of cruel and inconsiderate suppression by the British. Otherwise it would be a cowardice attitude to accept and surrender to the barbaric, unkind force and coercion of the foreign management.

In his social and political concept, nationalism is not a narrow and aggressive idea. Nationalism is a necessary stage in the social and political evolution of man and for the establishment of the human unity.

Aurobindo was against colonialism. When the First World War broke out, he said that it would mark the end of colonialism and the reawakening of Asia which was for him a very important step forward. He pointed out that German militarism was led by narrow ego and Aurobindo was very much against this type of narrow egoism or nationalism. Violent freedom struggle may fetch/bring political freedom which is significant for the comprehensive and entire development of the nation. Compatible with the very Indian tradition, this violent means was the last resort for him; the failure of the moderate principles of the Congress leaders for a long time prompted him to suggest violence as the prime method for the war of independence.

Vinayak Damodar Savarkar (1883–1966)

The political and philosophical insight of Vinayak Damodar Savarkar reveals a strong sense of nationalism which indicates that a person should respect his territorial integrity and geographical sanctity of his national borders and he should be most willing to sacrifice for the protection of this national spirit and integrity.

As the British government was an alien power, its rule or possession over India was absolutely contrary to this concept of nationalism and for the protection of this nationalism freedom struggle was inevitable.

Savarkar expresses the view that non-violence cannot be a proper method for solving our social and political problems where the opponents do not believe in the same method and language. Again, violence is not also desirable; violence can be adopted only as the last resort and as a relative and not as an absolute term. In the British India, he holds, national freedom movement should be in the violent means as the imperialists were not agreed to leave India following moral, non-violent principles. This view is quite compatible to the non-aggressive traditional Indian view.

Savarkar thinks that participation in the Second World War will pave the way for an opportunity of military training for the Hindus. So, he recognizes the significance and importance of the military training and violent method for the freedom struggle.

Savarkar's interpretation of Indian history clearly indicates that for the national cause and interest violent means may be embraced/adopted in war. He is opposed to the principle of unreasonable forgiveness and he severely criticizes the Buddhists for this unnecessary forgiveness which drives back Indian independence. He encourages violence in war and freedom struggle for the preservation and protection of the national culture and heritage. In his analysis of Indian history the foundation of the Marāṭhī power is considered as one of the six glorious epoches of the Indian history. Aggression against the enemy and not merely defence was the policy of the Marāṭhā leaders. As Savarkar considers it as a glorious chapter of the Indian history, his view shows that aggression and not always mere defence should be the appropriate policy in war for the national interest.

Savarkar views the so-called Sepoy Mutiny of 1857 as the first war of Indian independence. He admires the heroes of that struggle. According to him, the destruction of god-given liberty and imposition of political slavery motivated that struggle. It was not a mere military mutiny but a national and religious war. So, again for the national liberty and national cause he supports violent method in war.

Savarkar opines that in a perfect world absolute non-violence may be followed, a world which is full of saints and angels does not require violent methods. But in this imperfect world righteous violence in war is quite justified for the preservation and establishment of justice. He writes:

> We do not hold the justice which gives the death sentence responsible for bloodshed but rather the injustice which is taken to the gallows. Therefore, the sword of Brutus is holy. Therefore, the Bāghnakha of Shivaji is sacred. Therefore,

> the bloodshed in the revolutions in Italy is of fair fame. Therefore, the beheading of Charles I is a just deed. Therefore, the arrow of William Tell is divine.[6]

Savarkar's view is quite similar to Realism, one of the three traditions of thought dominate the ethics of war and peace. Realism maintains a skeptical attitude towards the application of moral concepts, such as justice, to the key problems of foreign policy. The realists claim that power and national security motivate and inspire states during a war and so moral considerations become strictly a wishful thinking. Talk of the morality of warfare is a pure bunk; ethics has got nothing to do with the rough-and-tumble world of global politics, where only the strong and cunning survives. A country should tend to its vital interests in security, influence over others, and economic growth and not to moral ideals.

The political philosophy of Savarkar expresses the view that the territorial bond (*rāṣṭra*), i.e. the attachment to *rāṣṭra* is a primary and fundamental criterion for being a Hindu. For the conservation of the liberty of this state or *rāṣṭra,* war is necessary and this war may be violent, for patronage and preservation of the liberty is a part of justice and for the justice violence may be adopted.

His nationalism is not narrow at all. His philosophy comprises humanistic, international and universal consciousness.

Quite compatible with the Indian tradition, Savarkar expresses the view that nationalism is significant but not the ultimate aim. The ultimate end is humanism or human unity. So, his philosophy encompasses humanistic attitude and international consciousness. Again, he believes that if a conflict can be solved by co-operation with the opposition, then there

---

[6] V.D. Savarkar, *The Indian War of Independence of 1857*, p. 274.

is no question of non-cooperation. But where non-cooperation is inevitable it must be followed, whether peaceful or violent. So, his philosophical attitude is not aggressive in nature.

His philosophical consideration indicates that victory in war entirely depends on the power and material strength. So, one who wants to win must be powerful. He remarks:

> We therefore say that people should not remain under any illusion that because their cause is just they are bound to win. Nothing can be more deceptive. If you want success in the world you must gain and improve your material strength. That is the only sure way to achieving success and to defeating your enemy.

One may be just, but if he is not considerably powerful he can never win. The Aryans won over their enemies because they were better organized and more materially advanced than their enemies. The reason for defeat of Pauras was his disorganization as well as the superior arms of Alexander. However, Candragupta wiped out the memory of any defeat by Alexander by his superior material power and military discipline. In 1857, Indian war of independence, though the causes of the Indian rebels were just, due to lack of proper power they were defeated and severely treated by the British.

So, power is quintessential for victory. In the empirical world victory is more associated with the concept of power and not so much with the justice–injustice issue. A just but weak one may be easily defeated by the unjust, if he is a materially superior opponent. But Savarkar says that power should not be aggressive or tyrant in mature though it is inevitably required for the conquest.

Savarkar analyses the seventh-century Islamic history and comments that power and material prosperity were the imperatives for their victory; might is right and that is the law of nature. This practical point of view proves that Savarkar was a realist thinker.

He repeatedly says that we should be aware of the competence, force and energy of our enemies. In Indian freedom struggle, moderate and militants were not concerned about the power of the British government. Only the revolutionaries were aware of that strength. His practical and realistic view regarding war situation is revealed here.

Savarkar opines that "might is right" is the principle of world politics. Power should not be employed to oppress others, but to save ourselves from the oppression of others. Analysing the contemporary world scenario Savarkar says that in spite of their bravery, moral and religious superiority Abysinia was defeated by a more powerful Italy. Again, though China had huge population, territory, firm religious conviction but they lost the battle to strong and impregnable military power of Japan. "Might is right" is the law of god and nature, and martial power is inevitable for self-preservation.

By anatomizing and interpreting the concurrent world politics and war situation, Savarkar points out that there are no permanent friends or foes in world politics. There is a difference between ideal and reality. International politics and war situation are more concerned with the reality and not with the ideal. Indian war of independence should be in accord with the world situation and hence it must be concerned with the real scenario and not only be engaged in ideal principles. This view reveals a very rational, pragmatic concept and opinion.

Savarkar comments and conjectures that for her own benefit, security and interest, and for the achievement of freedom, India must try to exploit the present international political situation. Realist perspective of Savarkar's view considers security as the principal concern of states and its absence the principal cause of war. It assumes security dilemma, polarity, power transition, etc. are responsible for acute conflicts. War is a situation which arises from unavoidable imperatives. Anarchy of the international system generates insecurity and prompts states to arm themselves and prepare for war. Savarkar's view is a defensive realism for due to the anarchy of the international system and the security dilemma it creates, Savarkar assumes security as the first propriety. His concept of war also can be treated as classical realism because he also stresses on the ethical perspective of war-issue. Classical realism intends to serve as a normative guide and to highlight the connections between ethics and successful foreign policies. It stresses sensitivity to ethical dilemmas and the practical implications and the need to base influence, wherever possible, on shared interests and persuasion. It recognizes the central role of power in politics of all kinds, but also its limitations and the ways in which it can be made self-defeating.

His practical war policy indicates that to win a battle one may have an effort to secure an advantage from the world political scenario. In our national interest we may hate others and may be engaged in killing and violence. It is not true that if we abstain from violence, killing and hatred then others will also give up and refrain from all these. In later period his view is ascertained as a real perspective in the case of Iraq–Kuwait relation. Iraq and Kuwait are neighbours. During the Iran–Iraq war of 1982-89 Kuwait offered substantial monetary help to Iraq. There is no historical reason for any animosity between the two. Yet Iraq invaded Kuwait in 1990 and committed barbaric atrocities on Kuwaiti civilians including women.

Savarkar expresses the view that military strength is necessary for the existence of a country, even for a democratic country; otherwise democracy will not be flourished and effective.

Savarkar opines that in the then state of human development passive resistance is practically unacceptable, though it is not entirely meaningless. He remarks that for the attainment of freedom, passive resistance is not at all a congenial or satisfactory method for the Indians. Passive resistance does not succeed unless it is backed by the force of arms. Without power, freedom could not be achieved. Mere passive resistance could not change any government which has financial and martial power. Savarkar thinks that passive resistance certainly is a noble principle but without the assistance and reinforcement of force of arms it would not succeed.

In his political thought Savarkar clearly asserts that violence is not the sole means for acquiring freedom. But in his contemporary subservient India there is no alternative to it. So, the revolutionaries follow this violent way. In his book *My Transportation for Life,* Savarkar stresses that if the British would allow political progress by peaceful means, he would reject armed struggle. He comments:

> It is rare to find a true patriot and humanitarian who would indulge in reckless and bloody and necessarily outrageous Revolution. — *My Transportation for Life,* p. 399

Savarkar points out that humanity is the highest principle and he detests violence. His non-aggressive and practical view proclaims that the revolutionaries adhere to or pursue violence under necessity and not by choice. The realistic war philosophy of Savarkar is "change according to times and plan new tactics". So, if violence is essential it must be adopted. The revolutionaries are not aggressors and they are fighting for a magnanimous/noble end. Those who capture other nations by force are the true aggressors. Violence is justifiable and defensible when it is practised in good cause and then it may be termed as true non-violence because in the long run it would reduce the unjust violence.

Savarkar closely observes that though without arms one cannot win a war, wars cannot be won by arms alone. Hitler conquered European nations like France, Norway, Holland and Belgium. These nations were defeated despite having arms because Hitler was more powerful. So, as a practical war tactics, it is necessary for a country to become more powerful than its enemies for the victory in a war.

Savarkar supports violent agitation against the British for a very practical reason. British government is unwilling and has no intention of granting independence to India. So, an armed uprising is unavoidable and destined in the then India.

The practical war philosophy of Savarkar manifests that in a war situation, any behaviour or virtue may be considered as praiseworthy or honourable in one circumstance and not in other. One must give due consideration to the relative strengths and weakness, circumstances, possible movements of the opponents for a war should not only be praiseworthy but also must be effective and achieve the desired end.

War principle of Savarkar makes a distinction between sacrifice and killing. Sacrifice is made for the benefit of others; it is made for a nobler cause than for self-interest. But killing is made for selfish intentions. In a war a good General intends to win a battle with the least casualties, and dying for the sake of dying is madness. Victory is the ultimate aim of a struggle and a good war policy must ensure maximum damage to the opponent with least damage to ourselves. Martyrdom may be a part of battle strategy but must be used in exceptional cases for it does not guarantee success.

Savarkar opines that violence is acceptable only in some special circumstances. It is not the only and ultimate end. Conspiracies, armed insurgencies, terrorism, defying the rule of law, sedition — all such activities are justified when overthrowing an alien rule is to be accomplished. But once the independence is won, we must consider such activities as sinful and abandon them immediately; otherwise they would boomerang and destroy our freedom.

Savarkar has faith in or reckons with humanity. Humanity or humanism is compatible with or consistent with the principle of non-violence and not at all with the violence or aggression. Savarkar repeatedly stresses and asserts that if the desired end can be achieved through non-violence and peaceful process then violent method is entirely dispensable and unjustified. So, maintaining the traditional Indian view he considers violence merely as the last resort though Savarkar approves, encourages and patronages violent or turbulent revolutionary movement for the Indian war of independence. So, an antagonism or conflict is cropped up/come into being between the ideology, i.e. faith in humanity, non-violence and the practical state situation. This kind of conflict is quite conventional and usual to Indian political concept on war and surprisingly it does not involve any logical contradiction. Ideologically Savarkar supports and reinforces humanity and non-violence and approves violence from the practical point of view and practical scenario. He asserts that "might is right" and for the victory in war as well as the attainment of justice power is inevitable. The principle of universalism has a significant role and contribution in this sphere. Humanity is certainly a good and fair ideal but this ideal will be accomplished and effective in the practical world if it involves universal element within it. Indian war of independence is entirely devoid of this principle of universality because the British authority has no faith in humanism. Lack of or non-existence of universality in the humanity ideology is a common feature of all the war situations of the world and due to this absence of universal acceptance, violence and power become obligatory and mandatory to attain justice. But this principle of violence and power is the last resort in the political reflection of Savarkar. Therefore, without the universal acceptance, the ideology of humanity cannot be effective in the pragmatic and empirical state-ethics or state situation and in that sphere violence is quite unavoidable for the attainment of justice and liberty. So, the conflict between humanism and practical state situation is natural and without any logical self-contradiction.

Conclusion

MODERN Indian concept on war manifests multifarious views like pacifism, realism, etc. though in the ultimate analysis it shows a harmonious ethical and metaphysical impression.

M.K. Gandhi's view is apparently pacifism and he is against of war. To him, war is unethical or unjustified because war accompanies means of violence and means justifies the end. Despite this, Gandhi approves and encourages Indian freedom struggle and this movement is also a kind of war, though in a different form. Gandhi himself is an eloquent figure of this war of independence. Gandhi encourages civil law on individual interests and so he believes that the sole purpose of the government is to protect the lives and property of its subjects which the British administration violates in India and so war in the form of freedom movement against this government is inevitable. This freedom movement is against the oppression and injustice of the foreign power; hence Gandhi patronizes it though in a complete non-violent form.

Gandhi supports Indian war of independence though in the non-violent way; hence he is not purely a pacifist. It is true that his war concept is different from the prevalent war concept. Customary or prevailing war concept considers violence as an indispensable element of war, whereas Gandhian philosophy prefers non-violent nature of war. To Gandhi, non-violence is a powerful weapon of war and this denotation and implication of non-violence makes his view non-aggressive. Gandhi believes in a very unconventional and distinctive power concept which indicates that true power positively contributes to the human welfare. This power is the power of truth and non-violence. This power is not attached with forced compliance or compulsion. Political authority is a real world fact though Gandhian philosophy is against any such authority in his ideal state. Political authority plays a significant role in the conduct of war. Political authority or state power takes care of the management of war. Hence, the nature of war, in many respects, depends on the nature of political authority which looks after the war.

Modern Indian political thinkers observe that in practice, democracies give their citizens only a very limited role in government in real scenario, in several occasions democratic state involves in a war without any consent of its citizens. Generally, a democratic state is considered as a welfare state which is concerned with the welfare of its citizens. So, it is assumed that when a democratic state involves in a war it should be aware of the less war devastation and it must not be attached with forced compliance.

War is a practical–real fact in the perspective of Indian political thinkers, specially in the views of Savarkar and Radhakrishnan. In this occasion they cite the instances of the ancient Greek city states which were diminished or declined not for their internal deficiencies but because of their external weakness in the face of invading armies. Hence, despite of being well-organized a state may be defeated due to its external weakness. As a real fact we cannot altogether refrain from the war situation.

In *Rāmāyaṇa*, King Rāvaṇa was more powerful than Rāma; but justice was with Lord Rāma and so he gained the victory. In the modern Indian concept, Savarkar's philosophy clearly portrays that in the practical world the question of victory is more intimately concerned with power concept rather than justice–injustice issue. Apparently, there is an ethical contrast between these two views though actually not. Rāvaṇa was powerful than Lord Rāma but that power was mere a material power. From the moral power aspect Lord Rāma was mighty or vigorous. Moreover, Rāma possessed advanced and eminent warlike skill which is a principal constituent for the victory. Savarkar points out that in the modern world some states have attained victory due to their material prosperity and improved military tactics though they are morally unjust. Therefore, not only the justice–injustice issue but morality or justice–injustice concepts along with the concept of advanced and powerful warlike skill contribute significantly to the victory in the warfront.

The concept of global justice involves respecting and protecting the basic human rights of people everywhere. In real–practical scenario, this respect and protection is not always secured; hence war is a practical fact. Human rights mark out genuinely universal features of human existence that transcend cultural differences. Human rights impose obligations of justice on us regardless of national or other cultural boundaries. It carries great moral weight. They correspond to the most serious kinds of harm that can befall a person. So, the violation of human rights necessarily leads to the conduct of war. Gandhi regarded the individual as the centre of authority and value. He held that the state and government derive their existence and power from the individuals. British authority violated human rights of the Indian people and national freedom struggle was inevitable in the outlook of Gandhi. Savarkar conceives that violation or contravention of human rights leads to a war. So, the war concept is intimately concerned with the concept of human rights and for the protection of these rights war may be inescapable or ordained.

A question may crop up that in a war the soldiers are killing their enemy and so they are violating human rights and right to life. But here we can resolve this issue by requiring that when the soldiers are fighting and killing the enemy in self-defence and for the national interest they are morally innocent and so the issue of violation of human right is immaterial and impertinent.

Both the terrorist acts and wars kill innocent civilians. Terrorist acts cannot be approved whereas modern Indian thinkers opine that war is permissible. A question can and should be asked here whether Indian view supporting war is justified or not. Here, in support of the Indian view it may be assumed that national interest and self-defence are absolutely absent in terrorist act and the Indian authorities support war and the violence of war only in the question of self-defence and the national interest.

Political–philosophical concepts of Gandhi, Savarkar, Aurobindo and Radhakrishnan express the view that the violation of human rights crops up war. The concept of national freedom is actually related with the concept of human rights. Without national liberty, human rights of the citizens can't be secured and protected. Violation of the human rights violates the inherent dignity of a human being. Human rights are the basic rights of a person which are essential for the realization of his personality as an individual as well as a member of the society in which he or she lives. Human rights ensure the necessary and vital protection of an individual so that he may continue his life and may contribute to the society in a dignified manner. Human rights cannot exist where economic exploitation prevails. In British India there are massive economic exploitations and oppressions which are not at all conducive for the preservation of human rights. Freedom struggle or national movement of Gandhi, Aurobindo, Savarkar is essentially a contrivance or means for the preservation of human rights. It clearly reveals that modern Indian concept on war is very much non-aggressive in nature.

Generally, in a war soldiers are permitted to attack the enemy at any time, whether they are attacking or not. They may attack enemy soldiers who are sleeping and present no current threat to anyone. Soldiers may attack military personnel whose role is not to engage in fighting, such as soldiers who transport equipment, repair vehicles or prepare food. If soldiers attack and kill them, the attacking soldiers are not acting in self-defence because they are not under attack. Though all these factors are generally permissible in war, modern Indian authorities repeatedly stress on the issue that from the perspective of human welfare and morality these factors must be reduced. They are conscious about diminishing and minimizing the horrors of war, human suffering and loss and this consciousness is reflected through their desires for protecting the civilians. Modern thinkers indicate that civilians are innocent people and they cannot be the legitimate targets of attack. So, their protection is a significant factor.

Political philosophies of Aurobindo, Savarkar, Radhakrishnan and Gandhi articulate/express the significance of national as well as global justice. Savarkar, specially, discusses and analyses this idea from a very pragmatic perspective. One very important requirement of global justice is that people everywhere should have the opportunity to be politically autonomous; that all political communities should enjoy rights of self-determination. Two factors can frustrate the search for self-determination. Either the political ambition of neighbouring states want to impose a form of imperial rule on the community in question, or an economic position that is so precarious that the community is given no real choices to make. Therefore the imposition of the imperial rule on one state by another violates the concept of world justice. To replace or regain this justice war may be indispensable.

There may be a conflict between different parts of the right to life. A debate may crop up — which should take precedence in conflicting situations? Is it the right of people not to be attacked or the right of people to defend themselves when their lives are threatened? Right to life assumes that if some state unjustifiably attacks another state, it has a right to defend itself from attack and to use lethal force if necessary. One's right to injure and kill the people of the other state may be justified on two grounds. First, by injuring or killing, one state can prevent the loss of the lives of its own citizens and second, in injuring or killing the attacker, a state can harm the other state who is responsible for the unjustified attack on the lives of its people. The right of self-defence permits us to harm the attacker because the attacker is responsible for the threat against us. By initiating the attack, the assailant loses his immunity, and the victim gains a right to kill the attacker as a means of defence. If there is no alternative means of self-defence, a victim has a right to kill the attacker.

Now the question is, whether the justification for killing the enemy soldiers in a war is compatible with the concept of human rights or not. The justification is that it is permissible for soldiers in a war to kill their enemy because the enemy soldiers are a threat and are responsible for their being a threat. Though the individual soldiers are not responsible for the war itself but they are certainly responsible for the threat which they impose on others whom they attack. Soldiers have a right of self-defence and this right permits them to kill the enemy soldiers who are attacking them.

The idea of human rights has been steadily in influence since the United Nations endorsed, in 1948, the Universal Declaration of Human Rights. But the concept itself can be traced long back, to the idea of natural rights that played a central role in the earlier stages of liberal political philosophy and which holds that all men at least have natural rights to life, liberty and property. So, as a natural right and certainly as a human right, liberty must be protected and to cherish or conserve this liberty, war — whether external or in the form of national freedom movement — may be destined or unavoidable. Without liberty one cannot lead a decent human life. Liberty or freedom is a very important political value.

Long-standing tradition views justice as central to the justification of political authority. Justice is of cardinal importance to a good government. Indian people were facing oppression in British India and there was no justice. Indians were not treated in a non-arbitrary way and they were not treated equally. On this very basis, British government was not a good government and it had no justification as a political authority. Hence, to extirpate this authority war in the form of freedom struggle is quite justified. Just society or a just political authority must give each member the most extensive set of basic liberties. British authority prevents the Indians from enjoying all these basic liberties and rights. Indians are denied the basic freedom. So, war against the British is fairly justified.

Global justice is an increasingly important factor in world politics. Just terms of interaction between nation states consist of a set of conditions. States must follow the treaties and other agreements they have made, they must respect one another's territorial integrity, they must not use force against another state except in self-defence and so on. So, for the self-defence one state may be involved in war and it ultimately ensures the global justice. Concept of war in Savarkar's philosophy repeatedly emphasizes on this aspect of war and global justice.

Power is, no doubt, essential in politics. One may argue that in international relations the concept of state sovereignty does not require power. For example, a few states, such as Liechtenstein and San Marino, have virtually no power at all, so far as international relations are concerned, yet they have sovereignty. But actually in these cases their sovereignty depends on the good pleasure of other states and undoubtedly they would not remain so if powerful neighbouring states chose to invade them and take over. Modern Indian political thought on war; specially the views of Savarkar, Aurobindo, Radhakrishnan reveal/transpire that sovereignty consists in supremacy of power. A sovereign state requires sufficient power to formulate and carry out its policies without having its freedom of action limited by any other body capable of exercising power. Power is inevitable for sovereignty and without proper freedom the enjoyment of power and sovereignty is not possible for a state.

In politics, it is obvious that mere power is not enough for an authority; both power and the acknowledgement of authority ensure a willing or at least an uncompelled obedience. In the relations between man and man, no one is there like god who can employ and exercise irresistible power everywhere and all the time, hence in politics only power is not adequate. Modern Indian political concept clearly manifests that when British or any other foreign power invades and occupies another state, they certainly possess power though they are without any acknowledgement. Since, man to man relation is not irresistible like god and because of that the authority of this foreign power may be confronted and war is a prime way for such challenges. This war may be an external war or a war in the form of national movement. Hence this war attitude is entirely or purely non-aggressive.

In British India, people were obliged to obey the British government only because they could be presumed to have tacitly promised obedience and to be morally obliged through that promise. They made the presumptive promise through fear of being killed and oppressed, so that the promise had been extorted by force. But without the promise, there would be no obligation and no dominion. Although the control of coercive power usually causes people to acknowledge a claim to authority, it does not always do so. So, if the nature of power is brutal and unjust, people may refuse to acknowledge the claim to authority and prefer to resist the power though the chances of successful resistance are slight. So, war of independence against such authority is quite justified.

The term "power" generally means ability. In the social context, this ability is a specific kind of ability, the ability to make other people do what one wants them to do. A man may be able to get others to do what he wants, because he has the gift of the god, or because they trust him for his wisdom or his integrity, or because he holds a special office, or because he has the strength to make things unpleasant for them if they refuse. Political power involves all these and the last one is significant in the case of conflict.

Power is not always unpleasant or malicious; but power in the coercive form is offensive and deplorable. When an imperial power attacks and occupies another territory, this coercive power causes conflict between that imperial authority and the subservient state. Indian freedom movement against the British basically is a struggle against such conscription or brute force. In a war situation there is always a possibility of the application of coercive force from the superior power. The possessor of coercive power enjoys a right — right of recipience. This right is a right to receive something, a claim against someone else that he has an obligation to provide what the right-holder is entitled to receive.

Freedom is the highest value of human life and it must be something vital and positive. Freedom is the absence of restraint on doing what one chooses or what one would choose to do if he knew that he could. Great value or influence of freedom is a part or essence of Indian philosophical thought and it is reflected in the concepts of Gandhi, Radhakrishnan, Aurobindo and Savarkar. Indian philosophical thought expresses that the mental or spiritual is real and the material is not. It is true that this concept is not directly relevant to social and political theory but Indian thinkers also hold that the end of human life is to realize the "true" or "higher" self. Self-realization is the ultimate value and freedom must have a close connection with self-realization. A man is truly free when he has realized his true self. Freedom is to be defined in terms of self-realization. Liberty is a necessary condition of self-development or self-fulfilment. Spiritual liberty as well as social and political freedom is required for this self-development. Social and political freedoms contribute to the expansion and manifestation of the spiritual freedom. Indian scholars believe that to attain this freedom national freedom struggle and external war may be inevitable.

Modern Indian political thought on war may be termed as consequentialism. Apparently, Gandhi's view appears as traditional absolutism. Traditional absolutism holds the view that "the taking of human life is always wrong" and the acceptance of it would commit one to absolute pacifism. But Gandhi supported national freedom movement because in British India human rights and justice were violated. Here, the traditional absolutism has taken the form of a different principle and the principle is "it is always wrong to kill innocent human beings". Gandhi and the other modern thinkers approved and encouraged war on the very basis of this principle. This philosophy denotes that war is permissible, since enemy combatants are not in the relevant sense innocent. Modern authorities patronage such a war situation where without approval of war innocent human beings will be tortured, oppressed and killed by the opponent. This different form or interpretation of the traditional absolutism supports consequential theory. War is permissible because in these situations without occurrence of war innocent people will suffer. So, this argument may be the one which comes most readily to hand to justify the waging of war.

Modern view is not aggressive for it considers war as the last resort. Here, there will be cases where the only way to resist aggression or oppression will be to engage in the war, i.e. the destruction of human lives (Gandhi's non-violent way is an exception); but the refusal to fight and to kill will be a failure to resist intolerable evil.

Modern Indian concept of war is a just war concept. Just war theory provides a set of criteria for judging when going to war is morally justified. It includes a just cause for war, legitimate authority to fight a war, reasonable probability of success, fighting as a last resort. It suggests to make a distinction between soldiers and civilians, and it prohibits attacks on civilians. Just war concept indicates that the damage done in achieving a military objective must match the value of the military objective in an appropriate way.

While discussing and analysing war theory modern Indian authorities emphasis on the legitimate and appropriate causes for war and these are security, protection of freedom, human rights, justice, etc. Their perspectives consist of valid authority to fight a war and the consideration of war as the last resort. External war as well as war in the form of national freedom movement is considered as the last option by them. They are deeply concerned with the attacks on the innocent civilians and the damage which war causes. Gandhi's preference for non-violence clearly justifies his concern and the philosophical insights of Radhakrishnan, Aurobindo and Savarkar confirm that the security and protection of the innocent people and the decreased or reduced war loss or damage are significant concerns for them. This principle may be considered as a version of the utilitarian principle which holds that we should always act to produce the best possible consequences. Modern Indian thinkers believe that the positive value of a military gain should be greater than the amount of harm that it causes. A war may be termed as legitimate which does not violate the rights of the people against whom it is directed. Unless and until one has lost his rights due to his own act, he cannot be threatened with war. Each and everyone has a right to life and other people do not have a right to attack them. But in the question of self-defence this concept of immunity to attack may be violated. When one is illegitimately attacked he can also attack and try to kill his attacker because he has a right to life and his self-defence demands this repulsion or counter-strike. But here, it is worthy to mention that the right to life of the illegitimate attacker is not at all violated because he has lost this right by his own act of unjustified attacks on others. Though Gandhi did not support this type of violent attack, he was justified in his opposition to the British on this very basis.

Modern Indian concept of war is not a revengeful attitude, but may be termed as a retributive principle. There is a difference between the two though the distinction between retributive and revenge is not always clearly recognized. Retribution only justifies the restoration of the moral balance disturbed by an immoral act, it does not justify the commission of a counter immorality. Modern Indian view of war is simply based on this retributive principle, i.e. its chief objective is the restoration of the imbalanced moral order. When some external power attacks or occupies our state then for the self-defence and national interest we must be in war and here war is imperative because other means than war have already failed. Attack from foreign nation and possession over our state creates an imbalanced ethical scenario and to bring back this moral order war is essential. Neither in the external war, nor in the internal freedom-struggle movement Indian perspective of war indicates to a revengeful action which is the mere satisfaction of a long-lasting feeling of ill-will resulting from a past insult or injury. This revengeful attitude merely possesses any ethical content. Indian war principle is a retributive principle and so after the re-establishment of the moral order (i.e. the rejection or refusal of the foreign invasion and the attainment of the freedom by the freedom movement) it does not suggest to hurt the opponent further.

Modern Indian concept on war may be considered as defencive deterrence as it approves war in that situation where one has no choice but to fight. It is true that this concept is not compatible with pacifism but it refers to the creation of a world where war is a less prominent feature and so it is not aggressive in nature.

Modern Indian philosophical perspective portrays non-aggressive attitude of war. Nationalism, national sovereignty, is vital and worthwhile. To preserve and secure nationalism war may be unavoidable but nationalism is not the ultimate goal but a necessary stage in the social and political evolution of the state. International consciousness and global human welfare stand as a concern and it reflects on the disapproval or disapprobation of narrow nationalism in the modern Indian evaluation and interpretation of war.

Modern Indian thinkers repeatedly emphasize on the national interest, but their concern is not confined to national interest only; they are also concerned with the interest and welfare of the citizens of the other countries of the world. Savarkar is a realist thinker, but like a pure realist he does not stress only on the national interest but a humanistic attitude and the welfare of the people of the entire world along with the national interest are considered significant in his philosophical approach. Modern thinkers believe that one has a predominant/initial duty to his own nation and he still has an auxiliary duty to the citizens of other countries. They have made a distinction between the fanatical preference of national interest and reasonable dedication to the nation's interest. It is a real fact that in international relations and in war situation people will certainly give a reasonable priority to their own country's interests and this priority, modern Indian authorities speculate, is quite compatible with the human consideration towards the other people of the world. There is no conflict between morality and self-interest. Morality does not indicate to the extreme altruism or a lack of concern about oneself or one's own national interest. Morality does not prevent nations from acting with self-interest, although it imposes restrictions and constraints on how this is achieved. Though there are sometimes conflicts between morality and the national interest, morality can also enhance the national interest. Modern thinkers assume that morality cannot be rejected, but at the same time, they endorse that abandoning and disregarding pragmatic consideration and the excessive focus on the moral perspective can create a negative effect.

4

War
Issues and Concerns in Western Political Thought

IN this present analysis an attempt will be made to expound the concept of war of the Western political thinkers. Attention of this presentation is basically focused on how the concept of war is related to the concept of state and the welfare of its citizens. Here, I want to explore the dilemmas of war and peace and the effects of the war on the state and society as revealed in the subtle and striking visions of the Western political philosophers. This presents a spectrum which ranges from Plato to Bertrand Arthur Russell — ancient to modern age — briefly reviews the views of Plato (427–347 BCE), Aristotle (384-322 BCE), John Locke (1632–1704), Immanuel Kant (1724–1804), Georg Wilhelm Friedrich Hegel (1770–1831) and Bertrand Arthur Russell (1872–1970).

Plato (427–347 BCE)

The present discourse is concerned with the concept of war of Plato as presented in his *Republic*.

Plato has dealt interestingly with the question of war. He asserts the importance of war in the management of state. According to *Republic* state and society are identical. Now, Plato confronts a very serious question that when the state will grow to a luxurious state, and is not large enough to support the original inhabitants what will have been the source to solve the increased demand for land. In such case Plato feels "that we shall be at war". He describes a single city-state, surrounded by others which are unreformed and by an outer-world of non-Hellenic nations. In this context the origin of war is in "desire", whether this source that is desire is the most fruitful source of evils both to individuals and to states is not a complicated question for Plato.

War is thus an art born out of the dire necessity because it is the question then of maintenance of a luxurious state needing the enlargement for its survival cutting of a slice of neighbour's territory. The justification of war is, thus, for the welfare of the state. The said welfare is expressed in the form of desire. As the war, for offence or defence, is a strong need for the welfare of the state, efficiency in the war is so important that its conductions are a matter of art. Thus war is an art because war or fighting is not a very easy task and a person of another trade, e.g. a farmer or a shoemaker cannot be engaged both in their professions and in war efficiently at the same time. The guardians, i.e. auxiliaries have to be chosen by their natural gifts and talents through a long process. Plato is thus the first to promote trained and educated professional soldiers to conduct war as an art for the welfare of the state. And because of the existence of the "spirited element" and the "sense of duty" and as "virtue is courage" — in the war, the war arising out of "desire" for the welfare of the state, the war is a necessity for the society also.

In *Republic*, another argument is advanced, while fight against foreign enemies means war, fight against same kindred, i.e. Greeks, is civil strife. Thus the foreigners, i.e. non-Greeks of other states or lands, are the natural enemy and fight between two Greek states is not like that in between the natural enemies, instead it is between the kindred people, so it is a civil strife and temporary in nature. In this point, Plato's approach is not devoid of a nationalist approach. This distinction shows that Plato considers all Greeks extended up to the borders of Hellas a race distinct from others as if it forms a commonwealth.

In question of the treatment towards the vanquished enemies Plato opines that it is mean and greedy in plundering a corpse, treating the body as an enemy is an expression of pettiness because when the spirit, the real enemy, has flown, leaving behind only the instrument, i.e. body with which he fought. It is to behave no better than a dog who growls at the stone that has hit him and leaves alone the man who threw it. Then he concludes that there should be no stripping of the slain and none should prevent their comrades from burying them. Instead Plato argues that all sides involved in the war should remember that the war will not last for ever; some day they must make friends again. It is fair that the victor should carry off the others, crops, but do no more. And it should not be forgotten that the whole populace against whom the victor have fought are not responsible for the quarrel but only a few of them. Therefore, the greater number of the populace is not enemies and as such their lands and houses should not be laid waste and destroyed. The citizens of a victor country should treat their adversaries and the foreigners in just like the way in which the Greeks treated one another. Plato proposes for the making of a law for the guardians, the law of not to ravage lands or burn houses.

Thus the *Republic* in this discourse, also, argues for some convention and rule for the treatment to be rendered to the soldiers and people of the vanquished enemies. The war conducted by the guardian class, whose fierceness in the characteristic of the spirited element in the soul and virtue from the education, is reflected in framing such laws about war. The conception of framing such laws is the result of the conviction that spirit needed to be tamed and controlled by the rational or philosophic element. War is needed for the state, i.e. society and the treatment to the enemies should have been done also with the spirit of the welfare of society.

Plato's such laws are the first signal for framing rules or laws in inter-state belligerency, i.e. conventional rules in the sphere of war devastations are first conceived and argued by Plato and it is emanated from the quest for justice.

Aristotle (384–322 BCE)

Here, Aristotle's treatment of the war-issue keenly follows his discussion of the state in *Politics*.

Politics refers to a very practical aspect of the *polis* (state) that strife and conflict are common features of the political community. At the same time he strictly asserts that political community must be concerned with the welfare of other humans, not just other citizens. From this universal humanistic attitude Aristotle speaks against war that to conquer and rule other territories lead to a violation of this freedom and the status as fellow humans. Despite this, Aristotle believes that defensive war is permissible and he suggests the establishment of a citizen militia for the defensive purpose.

Aristotle supports offensive war too in two specific cases — when a free community is under attack and needs help or intervention from outside and when a community cannot rule itself. Here, also, concept of human welfare inspires him to hold this view for Aristotle is quite confident that such intervention benefits the humans of that community and at least implicitly, the humans of the intervening community.

Aristotle points out that best government is that one under which man can act best and live happily. From this concept of "best government" it transpires that the happiness of the citizens is the end of the best government. If the happiness is the ultimate end of a government then a state or a government should not involve in a war unreasonably as it denies the happiness of its citizens. Certainly it is right that Aristotle approves defensive war but here also welfare of the state incites his consent. He encourages offensive war in two cases from the perspective of the prosperity and interest of the citizens. So, war can be approved only when it is beneficial to the state and its citizens.

Concept of state or society is enormously significant in Aristotle's philosophy. Without state or society man cannot exist. For the development and welfare of the state Aristotle endorses war. Man without law and justice becomes inferior and mean-minded and Aristotle admits the significant contribution of the law and justice in the case of state or society. Best state is that state where people can live happily and one can live happily where law and justice prevail. Unnecessary, aimless war violates law and justice and consequently defies and ruins the happiness of man. Hence, aggressive war is entirely unacceptable.

Aristotle opines that the wise state will necessarily regulate its citizens' life according to the best end and this best end is the human welfare or the welfare of its citizens. Hence, from this perspective, aggressive war that obstructs the welfare and interest of the citizens cannot be approved.

Aristotle criticizes the tendency of various communities — the Scythians, Persians, Thracians and Celts as well as the Spartans — to describe and represents war as admirable and to praise victory, domination and conquest. *Politics* (1324b1: 5-20) says:

> . . . in some states the entire aim both of the laws and of the constitution is to give men despotic power over their neighbours. And, therefore, although in most cities the laws may be said generally to be in a chaotic state, still, if they aim at anything, they aim at the maintenance of power: this

> is Laccdaemon and Crete the system of education and the greater part of the laws is framed within a view to war. And in all nations which are able to gratify their ambition military power is held in esteem, for example among the Scythians and Persians and Thracians and Celts. In some nations there are even laws tending to stimulate the warlike virtues, as at Carthaga, where we are told that men obtain the honour of wearing as many armlets as they have served campaigns. There was once a law in Macedonia that he who had not killed an enemy should wear a halter, and among the Scythians no one who had not slain his man was allowed to drink out of the cup which was handed round at a certain feast. Among the Iberians, a warlike nation, the number of enemies whom a man has slain is indicated by the number of obelisks which are fixed in the earth round his tomb; and there are numerous practices among other nations of a like kind, some of them established by law and others by custom.

In Aristotle's view, it is quite astonishing to think that a ruler should always consider how he can dominate and tyrannize over others. An unlawful matter cannot be the business of a ruler and the rule devoid of justice is certainly unlawful.

Regarding the origin of the state *Politics* indicates that when a number of villages are united and a single self-sufficient community is formed, the state comes into being. A state originates out of the bare needs of life and continues for the sake of a good life. Aggressive conflict is not at all conducive to such a good life.

Politics refers that security and welfare are the two central problems of the political life of a state. A state comes into existence for the establishment of a unperturbed life and its success and perfection lie in the installation of a good and beautiful life. So, aggressive war that hinders peace and prosperity of the state is not encouraged in *Politics*. The emergence of the state is for the life and existence of man, its manifestation is for an elevated and eminent life. Aggressive war that endangers the existence of state and human beings, is certainly, should be set aside or repudiated. His *Ethics* manifests the view that a real and true happy life is a life without any obstruction. War creates resistance in the political life of a state and this obstruction violates the possibility of a happy life.

Aristotle thinks that a man, separated from the state, easily involves in the madness/frenzy or inspiration of war. So, it indicates that in his view war should not be the natural disposition of man who is the part (citizens) of a state because security and welfare are the two significant elements of a state. It is decisively clear that Aristotle admits the utility and necessity of the defensive war for the bliss and good fortune of the state. Hence the question of the relevance of war is entirely related to the prosperity and happiness of the state in Aristotle's philosophy.

John Locke (1632–1704)

Locke's striking political–philosophical vision presents a spectrum which contains no concept of subordination or subjugation in the state of nature. This state is a state of perfect freedom and equality with a reciprocal power and jurisdiction. Justice, equality, charity, love, liberty, mutual duty are the features of the state of nature. Despite absolute liberty this state has no sanction for the destruction of oneself. Law of nature governs it which asserts that being all equal and independent no one has the right to abuse another's life, health, liberty and possessions. All men are the property of omnipotent, omniscient, perfect god and they have no right to destroy themselves as well as others. Everyone should preserve his own life and also the life, liberty and property of others. More specifically, "no one ought to harm another in his life, health, liberty or possession" (*Two Treatises* 11.6).

Law of nature, in Locke's philosophy is for the peace and preservation of all mankind and its violation necessarily demands the offender's punishment. State of nature recognizes the equality of all and there is no superior–inferior distinction in it. Being equal, here everyone has the right to punish the transgressor of law. This punishment is not to be driven by uncontrolled desires, rather calm reason and conscience have to dictate it and also to be expected proportionate to the transgression of law. In such sphere alone one can lawfully do harm to another. When one violates the law of nature he violates the rule of reason and equality that god has proposed for the common security of mankind and so the offender becomes dangerous for the existence and stability of mankind. Locke's view holds that defying the law of nature one disregards the rule of reason and a punishment is pardonable from the person injured or damaged for this transgression and for the restraint of crimes.

In the state of nature individual has no right to transgress the life, liberty and progression of others, and a war or conflict responsible for such transgression is certainly unfair. So, Locke speaks against the aggressive war here. Violation of the law justifies the punishment of the offender in the state of nature and the harm results from such punishment is the sole legitimate harm. Locke conceives that violation of the law effectuates the violation of equality and rule of reason, and for their preservation punishment is defensible. Such concept of the state of nature is compatible for the civil society too, though Locke does not say so explicitly, and to protect the law and rule of reason defensive war is permissible. Despite justification, punishment or war is to be dictated by controlled desires and conscience to get out of the way of evil outcomes of uncontrolled and unrefined passions. A transgressor of the law dishonours the rule of reason and in turn disobeys the liberty and equality of others. Here, a defensive war to preserve such liberty and equality is quite acceptable.

Locke speaks in favour of the right of self-preservation. In the state of nature, when one disregards the law of nature he actually violates the right to life and for the self-preservation, for the preservation of all mankind and for the restraint of crime, the transgressor has to be punished. Locke's view is that the person responsible for the unmerited violence and slaughter may be killed as that violence and slaughter against one are essentially war against all mankind. Indefensible violence renounces reason that is the common rule of god. Violating the law of nature one is no longer a part of the human society and human security, so he can be reasonably punished. Hence, defensive war is a valid and justified constituent of Locke's political horizon.

He observes that primarily men were in the state of nature and by their own consents they formed the society. Locke expresses his concern over the partiality of the executive power of the law of nature, possessed by everyone in the state of nature. He has doubt that self-love may ruin its impartial feature and individual may be driven by ill-nature, passion and revenge in punishing others. To keep clear of such partiality, violence, and the resulting confusion and disorder Locke prefers a civil government.

According to Locke, there are two core features of human mind — (i) liberty which considers will rather than force as the basis of government, and (ii) justice that means right, not might, as the fundamental feature of a political society.

Amidst being a source of enmity and destruction, defensive war is a reasonable and defensible concept in Locke's perception. It is quite rational to destroy one who threatens me with destruction. Preservation of human being is a fundamental principle and where preservation of all men is not a realistic concept, the safety and security of the innocent ones have to be preferred. When one makes war upon others he follows the rule of force and violence rather than the law of reason and he is then similar to a beast on its prey. Hence, a war against him who is dangerous to the human existence is justified.

When one intends and tries to get others into his absolute power without their consent he defies their right to freedom, tries to impose a design of his own choice upon their lives and makes them slaves. This is contrary to the law of preservation and so, here, a defensive war against that man is ethical and justified. Hence, Locke justifies war on the basis of freedom and self-preservation. Power-concept plays a key role in Locke's conviction of war. His observation reveals that those possessing absolute power over other's life, obvious outcome of which is the violation of the right to liberty and self-preservation, leading to conflict and antagonism. He who has absolute power not only dishonours other's right to freedom, but may further take away everything else by employing his force. War is against peace, good-will, mutual assistance and preservation, and it is concerned with enmity, malice, violence and mutual destruction. War is an application of force on one by another and to be relieved from that war against the aggressor though he (the aggressor) is in society and a fellow-subject is justified.

To escape from the war of the state of nature, men formed society where there is an authority with power that can resolve a tussle providing justice and relief. Power-concept has a significant role in Locke's philosophy of war. His conviction represents absolute power as a source of war that violates the right to liberty though he opines too that power may resolve the conflict. In the state of nature absolute power creates conflict. In a civil society an authority with power is expected to preserve human right and liberty and when it is corrupt war is indispensable. War is essentially concerned with power-concept. Power for the benefit and protection of human rights is good and enjoyable and has no role in the breaking out of war. A fair and deserved authority or power is a trust for the benefit of the people and it ensures their living and the enjoyment of rights; being corrupt it gives rise to war. Locke's primary contention is that the right to govern comes with a duty to govern in the interest of the governed. Failure by the government to recognize or observe this duty creates the right to rebel.

Natural liberty is free from any superior power but the law of nature. In society, liberty of man is under the legitimate power that they establish by consent. Freedom in the society is common to every member of that society which is not the subject to uncertain, unknown, arbitrary, inconstant will of other. Natural liberty is not under any restraint except the law of nature. In the same way, legislative power based on the consent of people solely controls social liberty and such power is to be necessarily just and good. Being corrupt, legislative power inevitably invites conflicts.

Locke's philosophy conceives freedom from arbitrary power as an essential element for one's preservation. One, not having the power of his own life is unable to enslave himself to anyone by his own consent or put himself under any absolute, arbitrary power of other to take away his life when he pleases. Other than himself, no one can assign more power to him and he who is not capable of taking his own life is incompetent to give another power over it too.

Locke's philosophical speculation denounces innate ideas of the rationalist approach and asserts experience as the origin from which moral principles derive. His concept reveals that moral principles may be certain.

He defines the concepts of good and bad with reference to pleasure and pain. Good is that which increases pleasure and diminishes pain, while bad or evil usually contributes in increasing pain and diminishing pleasure. Here, Locke's principle expresses a consequentialist idea. Locke declines the theory of the divine power of royal authority. In his view, force exercised without right, creates a state of war. Natural moral law is discoverable by reason. The state of nature is a state of liberty but not of licence. All men are the creatures of god. Though a man may defend himself against attack and punish aggressors on his private initiative, there is no common temporal sovereign or judge. Locke has a fair conviction in natural rights. Everyone has the right to preserve himself and to defend his life and has a right to his freedom too. There are certainly other correlative duties also. Having a duty to preserve and defend his life one has a right to do so and as he is morally obliged to take the means at his disposal to preserve his life, he has no right either to take it himself or by subjecting himself to slavery to give to another the power of taking it.

Locke's philosophical outlook views the right of private property as a key natural right. Man has a right and duty to preserve himself and it confirms his right to property that contributes to his protection and preservation. Attaching one's labour to something for removing it from its natural origin establishes one's right and possession over that thing. Though Locke admits the right to private property, he ensures its limitations too, created by the law of nature. He discourages and condemns the enjoyment of property that is detrimental to others.

In Locke's concept, society is not something unnatural to man. Civil or political society is natural as it fulfils human needs. Although men are liberal and they have some natural rights in the state of nature, in actual practice it is very hard to preserve and protect these rights and freedom as no common authority prevails there. Always men are not concerned with the equal rights of others and the observance of the common moral law though in ideal, they are compelled to do so. Hence, for the preservation of their rights and liberties and their own interests men have absolutely consented for fixing the lapses and the formation of an organized civil society. So, Locke's state of nature is not an ideal state for him.

Despite being rational, biased by their interests, men are not being all the times faithful and obliged towards the natural moral law. Again, men are usually overzealous in their own cause while deciding punishments for the transgressors. Here, the need for an established and commonly recognized judicial system and a written law to define the natural law comes up. In Locke's contemplation, the essence of society lies in the mutual preservation of the lives, liberties and estates of men that he calls "property".

Political society and government are based on a rational foundation and the consent of the people. Being rational, this society fulfils a useful purpose. The complete freedom of the state of nature is necessarily curtailed in the society and such curtailment is quite justified for this society is rational and based on the consent of the people. Such curtailment is justified because in a civil society men unite into a community for their comfortable, safe and peaceful living, secure enjoyment of their properties.

In reality, men do not renounce their liberty when they enter into a society. The form of the liberty in the society is distinct from that in the natural state. This different form in the society is essential for it ensures common good and the enjoyment of the liberty.

Locke regards federative power that makes war and peace. Though considering it as a distinct power Locke remarks that it can hardly be separated from the executive in the sense of being entrusted to a different person for this will cause ruin and disorder.

Political insight of Locke discloses the intimate relation between the society and its government. The dissolution of society necessarily invites the dissolution of its government and such dissolution by force is termed by Locke "overturning from without" (T.19, 211). Another type of dissolution, "dissolution from within" occurs while government acts contrary to the trust reposed in it, contrary to the life, liberty, property of the citizens.

When government is disintegrated, rebellion is justified. The citizens, exploited under a tyrannical rule, may go for a justified rebellion at the dissolution of that rule. Amidst the view that rebellion is justified, still Locke confesses the possibility of unjustified rebellions that are nothing but crimes.

Preservation of private property and common good are the two principal objects of the government and Locke stresses on the progression of economic life along with the social and political lives.

Locke denotes that his assertion of equality of all men in the state of nature is not the equality of all sorts. Age, virtue, excellence and merit may place one above the common level. In his view, equality of all men consists in equal right to freedom that without one's consent no authority can subject him.

In a civil or political society commonwealth has the power of law that contributes to the punishment of the transgressor. Again, while members of the society get injured by someone from outside, commonwealth has the right to punish him. This is the power of war and peace, and preservation of the property of the members of the civil society justifies it. Laws of the civil society are for the public good. Civil society is a remedy to the inconvenience of the state of nature that derives from anyone's power of being judge. In civil society, a common authority enjoys the judicial power, to which everyone may appeal.

Being rational one should enjoy liberty to judge and defend his right, asserts Locke. Otherwise he would have been exposed to all the misery and inconvenience that one can fear from other. Locke denies that absolute power purifies man's bloods and corrects the baseness of human nature. He is not in favour of absolute power. He speculates that no man in civil society can be exempted from the laws of it.

Locke has a very firm conviction that no one can be subjugated by another's political power and his property can never be seized without his consent. This perception is compatible with the concept of war. Locke is of the opinion that a country's political power has no right to subjugate other state through war and to seize the property of the defeated nation too.

Though men are absolutely free in the state of nature, equality of the right to freedom makes its enjoyment uncertain and constantly invites a possibility of invasion from others. Equality and the absence of an observer of equality and justice incite unsafe and unsecured freedom and right to property. This fear triggers off the formation of the society and reason inspires men for such a social organization.

In the state of nature all are equal, both judge and executioner of the law of nature. So, passion, revenge and partial perspective regulate and drive the human nature. Despite civil society or government is grounded on the consent of people, disordered ambition in the world denies the significance of such consent and thus conquest takes place.

An aggressor, unjustly invades other's right though he has no legal and fair right over the conquered. He can simply forcefully demand one's submission whom he conquers, still he cannot exert his legal right on him. One may appeal to the law of justice while a robber has stolen his property but the conquered ones have no court to appeal.

Locke presents a different view in the context of a lawful war. The conqueror of a just and lawful war has an absolute power over the lives of those who has fought against him unjustly as they are guilty of the violence and injustice committed in an unfair war. But the conqueror has no power and right over the lives of the innocents who have no participation in the unjust war. While the conqueror possesses a power over the lives of the conquered ones engaged in an undeserved and unreasonable war with him, still he has no right over their possessions. So, his power is purely despotic in nature.

Locke's philosophy expresses concern about the protection and preservation of the innocent people that resembles the Indian view of war. Though violence is employed in both just and unjust wars, people engaged in unfair war are condemned of violence and the conqueror of a just war, although applying violence in a war is free from being guilty of making use of violence. It transpires that in Locke's view violence is not itself good or evil. It is fair or unfair due to its way of application. His philosophical perspective reveals that life and property or possession are entirely distinct concepts. The right over one's life necessarily not involves the right over his possession.

War involves force and damage. Unfair and unmerited force sparks off war. Reason rules the world of men while force guides the animal world. Making use of the unjust force one involves into war reducing himself to the status of a lower animal who losses his right to life and becomes liable to be destroyed by one against whom he uses the unjust force. Locke's observation reveals that reason induces individuals entering into social organization while again relinquishing reason, rational men engage into aggressive war and employ force.

Involving into an aggressive war while one administering

unjust force he loses his right to life and the right of conquest extends to his life though not to his estate. Confiscating his property involves application of unjust force similar to robbery. Conqueror has no right to take away more than the defeated could forfeit. The family (wives and children) of the vanquished has a right to his possession and the humanitarian, rational and pragmatic perspective of Locke's philosophy firmly condemns the violation of such right of the innocent people.

While an aggressor conquers and imposes force on the vanquished against whom he had no right of war or who joined not in the war against him, he had right, has no obligation upon them. Conqueror has no absolute or arbitrary power over the life and liberty of the innocent people of the vanquished country. Without their consent conqueror has no lawful authority that compels them to submission. He has no right to the land and people of the conquered country.

Locke's assertion is that everyone has a double right. First, a right of freedom and no other person has a power over it. Second, a right to inherit his ancestral property.

By the right of freedom, a man is naturally free from subjection to any government, though he is born and lives in a place under its jurisdiction. Locke asserts that declining the lawful government of the country which is his birthplace he loses his right that belongs to him by the laws of it and the right to his ancestral property too, while such any government made by their consents.

Despite a promise of granting something to other for ever while one claims that he has right, if he pleases, to take it away from him again, it reduces to a ridiculous matter. It confirms that there is no free and voluntary contract and such any contract may be dissolved any time by mere power; all the grants and promises of men when he is in power are nothing but mockery and collision.

Locke has a conviction that a king is surely a subject to the laws of god and nature. No power can exempt him from such an obligation of the external law.

In his view on war, concepts of right and liberty have vital denotations. Where one violates the right of others by getting into his possession, it is usurpation that shows taking a position of power illegally or by force. Locke clearly condemns unjust and unlawful force.

Applying force upon the people without proper authority that goes contrary to the trust put in him who makes use of the force brings about a state of war and reduces him to an aggressor.

Locke observes that the dissolution of the society necessarily invites the dissolution of the government. Society that provides dependence and protection from violence often is sustained a loss from a conqueror that injures protection and dependence of the people. Being intimately related, loss or damage to a society which is the root of a government triggers off the dissolution of the government itself.

Locke considers despotic power as an absolute, arbitrary power of one over another to take away his life whenever he pleases. Nature or social contract does not sanction such power. No one possesses this arbitrary power over his own life and cannot give other to employ it over his life too. Only the life of an aggressor is the subject of that power as involving in an unjust war he himself forfeits his own life.

Reason is the rule which naturally regulates man to man relation and the establishment of peace. While renouncing reason, an aggressor administers force on others, though he is not merited with that right, to satisfy his unjust end.

Locke perceives god as the supreme judge of the right, still his view refers every man as judge for himself. He completely entrusts moral responsibility on man and to him war is determined by human beings, not by any other condition.

The ruler of the commonwealth is bound to govern following the established laws. He has to prevent or redress the injuries and evil consequences from a foreign invasion and secure and protect his community from invasions which reveals that peace, safety and public good are the chief ends of the ruler. Foreign invasion is not compatible with peace and safety of the people. Aggressive war from other countries is contrary to the public good, prosperity and safety of the country invaded and for all these, it is irreplaceable to prevent invasion.

Locke emphasizes on the significance of law and comments that tyranny begins where law ends. When an authority exceeds his law-abiding power and applies his force incompatible with law he remains no more a proper ruler and deserves an opposition as justified. One who forcefully invades the right of others must be opposed. Someone rich and rightfully possessing great power has no right too to oppress others. Oppression and invasion against the innocent people, not involved in an unjust war, are indefensible or unfair.

Applying force, while one threatens other's life and where the person attacked has no sufficient time to take advantage of law he may justifiably killed the invader as law has no power to restore life to one's dead carcass and such loss is irreparable. Law of nature permits one the right to prevent a person who is responsible for his destruction, he may rightfully destroy him. But where life is not endangered and the loss is reparable by law, no need for destruction, Locke confirms. His thought acknowledges defensive war and the killing of assailant for the preservation of life though his perception is non-aggressive. In self-defence killing is justified. Defensive war is the war against injustice for the protection of life and property. Both in the lives of individual and the state defensive conflict is permissible. Law of nature allows defensive conflict and social laws are conducive to it too.

Establishing society and civil government men cast off force and frame laws that have conformity with peace, property and unity. Whenever defying law an authority again tries to administer force state of war is effectuated. Locke observes that force without authority generates war. Introducing a power by a ruler devoid of authorization of people provokes war. Illegal attempts on the liberties or properties of the people and unlawful violence bring on bloodshed. Invasion of the rights of people by force causes conflicts. Locke's speculation is that those who employ force or power without having an authority are the enemies of the mankind.

Everyone has a right to defend himself and to resist the aggressors. Nature allows freely to all other creatures as well as human beings "opposing force with force" for their preservation from injury. Self-defence is a part of the law of nature. To resist force with force or the war situation negates all former relation of reverence, respect and superiority, and that he who opposes the unjust aggressors has this superiority over him, that he has a right, when he prevails, to punish the offender both for the establishment of peace and to eradicate the evils.

Locke speaks of peace and preservation of all mankind in the state of nature. Everyone has to protect his own life, and the life, liberty and property of others too. Such universal concern for mankind essentially is not compatible with aggressive attitude. War involving transgression of life, liberty and passion of others is unjustified though he sanctions defensive war for the preservation of law and rule of reason that encompasses equality and liberty with a controlled desire and conscience. His firm belief in self-preservation and right to life reveals equality, liberty and property as essential for its conservation. Self-preservation again justifies defensive war while one threatens other's life. Unethical or unauthorized power or force creates war violating right to life and liberty. In state of nature, absolute power creates conflicts. In a civil society an authority with power is established with the expectation that it would preserve human rights and liberty. Hence, in Locke's philosophy power is not necessarily an evil concept. Power, with uncontrolled passions, only creates war. Human nature is like that vested interests and jealousy often hijack the transgression of law and rule of reason and precipitate war. Though civil society has a rational basis and consent of people, still power-concept, force, vested interest, jealousy result in war and conflict. Men consented for the curtailment of their liberty to some extent for the formation of a civil society to escape the conflicting scenario of the state of nature, though in reality still they are confronting war and violence.

Locke's consequential moral principle transpires that aggressive war is indefensible as it results in evil consequences like transgression of law, equality and liberty; peace and progress. Uncontrolled self-interests, concerned with the brutal and ruthless nature of the aggressive war, invite increasing sufferings of men. Though defensive or lawful war causes devastations and losses, still it gives rise to much more fair and good consequences. It stimulates law, peace, liberty and equality in the society with a controlled rational desire. Concern for the lives and wealth of the innocent civilian people of the vanquished nation asserts its rational, humanitarian nature.

Immanuel Kant (1724–1804)

In his political philosophy, discussing the international relations Kant represents his view that if the freedom of a state is threatened by the action of the other state then right and law cannot prevail. For Kant, concept of right is immensely significant and the abolition of war is necessary for the establishment of the right and freedom of the individual.

Kant explores the distinction between the natural world and the human world. Nature involves the war of all against all whereas men are free, equal and self-dependent. The possibility of war can be diminished only in a civil society because the bindings of law prevail there. Freedom of an individual can be protected only by his compliance to coercion which is presupposed by law. Since, freedom is Kant's principal value, coercion is allowed only where it is both necessary to preserve freedom and possible for it to do so. From the ultimate value of freedom, Kant derives the universal principle of justice, that an action is right only if on its maxim the freedom of choice of each can coexist with everyone's freedom in accordance with a universal law. Kant then points out that coercive legal enforcement is justified when it can prevent a hindrance to freedom. Coercive enforcement of the law does not prevent freedom, for the threat of judicial sanction does not deprive a would-be criminal of freedom in the way that his crime would deprive its victim of freedom: the criminal exercises the choice to risk sanction, but deprives his victim of freedom of choice. Political freedom is an autonomy which is devoid of coercion by another will. All individuals must be equally free for their freedom is absolute and only law can equally and universally restrict this freedom.

Equality is the second principal right of a citizen in a state. Each and every individual is equal before the law and there should not be any exception. This equality is political equality; Kant here does not refer to the economic issues and equality. But in his writings he emphasizes on the right of individual to own property and the economic independence as a criterion for active participation in the political affairs. For Kant, the right to property is not a natural right of isolated individuals, but a social creation depending upon mutual acceptability of claims. The state exists primarily to make claims to property rights, both determinate and secure, and anyone claiming property rights thus has both the right and the obligation to join in a state with others. The free citizens of a state must also be self-dependent, i.e. they must have the right to take part indirectly in the administration through the election process.

War or the preparation for war endangers the rights of man. The citizens of a state are not safe unless there is a stable and peaceful environment. Safety and security of the citizens are intimately concerned with the peaceful relation between different states. The ultimate consequence of war is the death and annihilation of all which is quite relevant in the present nuclear age of total war.

Kant here offers a positive solution though it is unrealistic. The establishment of a cosmopolitan society or a world state can reduce the possibility of the conflict, though all the states will not agree to surrender their sovereignty and to be administered by a world government or a supreme authority.

In this context, Kant also suggests a negative solution that war is too expensive and the citizens of the concerned state have to bear this economic burden, hence, they do not desire war any more.

Kant proposes the concept of a federation of states which opposes war. War is not the proper means of resolving disputes between states. Showing respect for the law, Kant here opines that law can solve the international disputes.

He severely criticizes the principle of expediency in international affairs. He analyses and disapproves the view that "might is right" which is the origin of expediency. The principle of expediency is an obstacle for the perpetual peace. This is uncertain and imprecise and not an a priori principle of right. It does not involve reason and any philosophical enquiry into politics.

Kant delineates that the real problem of politics is to ensure right that is law and justice. He condemns rebellion as it violates law and it creates anarchy and violence. It is improper to overthrow the ruler for it does not lead towards a true reform of thought. If the citizens are oppressed and their happiness is taken away then also they have no power or right to rebel. Certainly, Kant thinks that obedience or humble respect are not synonymous with silence and not the rebellion, but the rational open criticism, in his opinion, is the proper way for the protest and expression of the views of the citizens.

Kant expresses the view that there is a crucial, sharp distinction between the concept of peace and the temporary suspension of the conflict. Peace involves the end of all the future possibilities of war. The end of a particular war does not simply ensure peace, i.e. it does not invalidate all the present reasons for another future war. If the consistent increase of the power of a state is considered as the form of glorification for a state, the confirmation of peace is certainly impossible. Here, Kant opposes and criticizes the principle that a state can augment its capabilities and power by any means for its glory. Increasing power is not an indication for the prosperity and development of a state. This view is quite relevant for our contemporary world which is severely struggling against the abuse of power and for peace.

An independent state should not be acquired by some other state by inheritance, exchange, purchase or gift. State is a social human organization, it has its own roots, tradition, culture and to graft it on to another state endangers its existence just like a tree. Here, Kant is concerned with the significance of own culture of a state; war and conflict are not at all conducive for this tradition and culture.

Kant is decisively clear that standing army should be abolished as it always threatens the other states and creates a chance of war, which reduces perpetual peace to dust. Moreover, hiring of men to kill or to be killed converts them into mere machines or instruments in the hands of the state which is absolutely contrary to the rights of man. Apart from this, a state accumulating unlimited wealth may be considered as a war threat for the other states and they may proceed for a preventive attack. Kant here analyses and shows the economic interpretation of war and confirms that desire for boundless, excessive wealth and accumulation of it lead to conflict between different states.

He is of the opinion that a state can borrow money for its internal developments like improvements of roads, new settlements and storage of foodstuffs for the time of famine, but not for any aggressive conflict because it inevitably invites national bankruptcy and make perpetual peace a mere myth. Analysing the human mental world Kant opines that warlike inclination is an integral feature of the nature of those who are in power. This is the psychological aspect of war. This warlike inclination, coupled with friendly and favourable circumstances creates war. When a state borrows money for some aggressive war against other states it appears as the "power of money in its most dangerous form".

Kant is quite unambiguous that a state cannot forcibly interfere in the internal matter (constitution and government) of another state on the basis of some pretence/excuse of scandal or offence against that state. Such interference may be considered as valid only if a state is divided into two parts due to some internal problem and consequently there is a possibility of anarchy. Apart from this, the interference from an external state violates the "rights of an independent people" and "autonomy of a state" which is a serious active offence. Kant, here, shows a great respect for the right of an independent individual and the autonomy of a state. The independence of the individual in face of authority and the problem of human freedom make a core area of Kant's political thinking. Principles of right are Kant's principles of politics. This is a highly moral as well as practical outlook and also certainly relevant in our contemporary world. In the recent past, the conflict between the US and Iraq, and the interference by the US was based on such charge of scandal and offence against Iraq.

The real problem of politics is to ensure right, i.e. law and justice. In Kant's view, justice is universal and political actions must be universal like ethics. Only law can bring this universal justice. The universal principle of right in Kant's philosophy is derived from the universal moral principle which ensures that the action which enables the coexistence of the freedom of one individual with the freedom of everyone else is the just action. If this coexistence is violated then the use of coercion, law must be employed, i.e. the use of coercive method is implied by the principle of right.

The employment of deceitful means such as assassination, poisoning, breach of agreements, the instigation of treason is a great obstacle in the way of future peace, going by Kant. The application of such means at war time creates distrust between two states but this mutual confidence is inevitable for the future peace. Kant's political observation shows that the ethical perspective of war involves fair means.

Kant explores a distinction between the human society and nature. Nature, he thinks, is "war of all against all" that is "a state of war". On the other hand, though the human society does not involve active hostility but there is a constant threat of its breaking out. Temporary suspension of such hostility does not ensure future or perpetual peace and so Kant's pragmatic suggestion is that peace must be formally instituted.

The civil society resists an individual from an arbitrary aggressive attitude towards others and law plays a significant role here. A state of lawlessness encourages arbitrary/ capricious attack and hence Kant lays emphasis on the civil society, law and constitution. This observation of Kant assimilates politics with ethics. For Kant, political theory is intimately associated with morality. Politics is concerned with our just treatment in social and political contexts and with the principle by which public conflicts of interests can be settled. Kant feels that our social–political issues and the public conflicts must be governed universally and this indicates to the necessity of law or legal system.

His political thought explores that all the free individuals have the right to acquire anything from the world of nature. But the conflict between the freedom of one individual to that of other must be avoided; the freedom of one should not obstruct the freedom of another; otherwise there will be chaos and continuous strife. Law alone can prevent this conflict and chaos, and not in a state of nature, but only in a civil society law can prevail. The individuals, who can physically influence each other, living in a mere state of nature, make war possible. Civil society and law can only prevent this. Certainly in the contemporary world all the wars are conducted by the authority of some civil society and state, but what Kant wants to convince is that the constraint of law in a civil society diminishes the possibility of conflict.

Kant believes that the republican constitution is the best one which can bring the perpetual peace. It is pure and based on the principle of right. This type of constitution demands prior consent of the citizens before the declaration of war and then the citizens, quite naturally, hesitate to give that consent by considering the evil consequences of the proposed war such as doing the fighting themselves, supplying the costs of the war from their own resources, painfully making good the ensuing devastation, and having to take upon themselves a burden of debt. In this context, Kant points out to a political principle that in a republican framework the ruler considers himself as a fellow citizen and hence, their consent is valuable and significant for him. But in the other cases, ruler appears as the owner of his state and not as the fellow citizen and so he is not at all concerned with the miseries and consent of his citizens; war cannot make slightest difference in his luxuries and war appears to him as an amusement. In Kant's view, for the prevention of war the ruler must have sympathetic attitude towards his subjects instead of being arrogant; he must remember that he has to protect the rights of men. This is a psychological aspect of the prevention of war. Republican form of government is based upon three principles — the principle of freedom for all members of a society, i.e. freedom is the possibility of acting in ways which do no injustice to others; the principle of the dependence of all upon a single common legislation; and the principle of legal equality for all. Republican state is to accord with the concept of right, so it prohibits violence and despotism; and Kant's political thought delineates that concept of right resists or obstructs violence and despotism.

Kant proposes for the establishment of a federation of peoples which may diminish the war possibility. This federation will ensure the security and the rights of each and every nation. Discussing the concept of war, Kant points out to a principle of the state formation which holds that lawlessness situation is a barbarism, coarseness and brutish debasement of humanity and the establishment of state and legal principles (law) is the only way for the emancipation from it. Kant is very clear that reason is the highest legislative moral power and it condemns war. His practical viewpoint asserts that peace will not be secured without a general agreement between the nations and the establishment of a federation. It differs from a peace treaty; peace treaty abolishes a single war whereas it terminates all wars for good. This federation does not try to secure power for a single state, leading to the perpetual peace, it rather tries to protect and secure the freedom of all the states. Kant's view confirms that for the perpetual peace, freedom of all nations and a non-aggressive attitude towards the acquisition of power are required. To prevent war, it is inevitable to renounce the lawless and savage freedom, the freedom of folly, and to adopt the public coercive laws which maintain the freedom of reason.

He opposes war and argues that no one has any greater right than the others to possess any particular portion of this earth and human world shares commonly the right to the earth's surface.

Kant reflects on the human nature that war seems to be ingrained in the nature of men and so, actually, it does not need any strong external motivation. Self-seeking inclination of human beings obstructs the establishment of the justice to the rights of man and leads to war. Every state desires to achieve lasting peace by thus dominating the entire world. But nature employs linguistic and religious factors which create mutual hatred and difference and leads to war possibility. A nation requires a strong commercial and financial background for its prosperity and development which can be ensured only by a peaceful state and war, certainly, defiles the spirit of commerce.

Kant is distinctly clear that the state authority should seek advice from the wise or the philosophers regarding the war-principle and for the establishment of peace. Here, Kant holds a view contrary to Plato that the philosophers should not be expected to be the rulers because possession of power definitely corrupts the free judgement of reason. Plato, on the other hand, instructs to make the philosophers as rulers because they have the control of senses which helps to restraint the corruption. Plato's philosophy affirms that there is no conflict between politics and ethics, i.e. between the theory and practice. Ethical ideas in the theoretical form, and when they are applied in politics, i.e. in the practical power contexts, can be in well co-ordination or can go together without any contradiction.

Kant analyses and explains the power-concept that if a state is powerful or superior than the others, it commonly takes an attempt to plunder the comparatively weaker state and to be engaged in war and possess it; it is no matter whether the other state is in its way or not. This war or conflict reduces the rights of the individuals into mere theory and impracticable principle. War is certainly and intimately related with the power-concept and this power-factor definitely causes war.

A state, which follows the mechanical workings of nature, not depending on the moral law or freedom, merely utilizes nature in needs of man that is for the government and then the concept of right cannot be established. This type of politics has no relation with morality. Kant suggests that a moral politician should try to correct the fault or conflict which is found in the political constitution or between the two states as early as possible. This correction is possible if politics conforms to the natural right and for this conformity selfish interest of the state as well as its individuals must be sacrificed. The complaisance between politics and ethics can reduce the conflict between states and ensure peace.

Kant analyses the psychology of the great state powers and states quite confidently that they are not ashamed of their injustice and not embarrassed about how the people and the other states will criticize and condemn them. They are only aware of their success or failure. Kant's view is that this psychological aspect of the great powers leads to the preparation for war.

He explores the nature of war and his view represents the importance of right in politics. A state authority, denying to respect the concept of right will be completely unjust and right alone is capable of establishing perpetual peace. A true political system must conform to morality. Political authority should consider the rights of man as sacred, even if it has to make a great sacrifice for that. Kant points out to the evil aspect of the human nature and states that this psychological feature of man makes coercion a necessary constituent.

Kant also disapproves and condemns the concept of rebellion. People have no right to rebel, he thinks. There can be no power to determine what constitutes the right to rebel. Rebellion disrupts the whole system of laws and it leads to anarchy and violence. It also violates the civil constitution. But Kant is of the opinion that if a rebellion is successful then to re-establish the old administration and to reverse the rebellion are wrong because then the position of the previous ruler is reduced to a mere subject and it is man's duty to obey and accept as citizen the newly-established government. Certainly it is true that Kant expresses the view that obedience is not mere silence and if the citizens realize that their happiness and freedom could be taken away they can go for rational and open criticism of the powers.

Kant feels that for the establishment of the international rights lawful condition is inevitable. It means that the external circumstances must be consisted of the application of the international rights.

It may be the case that a state becomes large and powerful in such a way that it creates fear of being attacked in the mind of its less powerful neighbouring states and this state may attack the other out of this assumed fear and uncertainty. Kant is very confident to condemn this as an unjust act. In his thought, a federative association intends to eliminate war and it is the only lawful arrangement. A federal union unites politics and morality and it gives a priority to the principles of right. Kant's view is distinct, crystalline that the philanthropy and respect for the rights of man are the obligatory principles which are not conducive to war. This view represents that war or conflict violates these ideals.

War–peace concept in Kant's philosophy is comprehensively organized by the concepts of right and freedom. These two concepts (right and freedom) are immensely significant for Kant. War can be prevented and minimized only in a civil society as there are law and coercion. Kant sanctions coercion only where freedom and right can be preserved by it. It appears that Kant's war-contrariety (opposition) entirely depends on his conviction of the necessity of right-freedom preservation. Kant's view represents that having a right to receive something implies a right against someone else, who has an obligation to provide that right to the former. Right of recipience is a right to receive something; it is a claim to something due. On the other hand, right of action is a right to do something and it indicates to the obligation on the part of someone else. The violation of this claim and obligation makes war or conflict inevitable and the constraint of law contributes to the preservation of such claim and obligation. The principle "might is right" leads to war. For the peace, Kant opposes this concept. Analysing power-concept, Kant shows that it is not fair or justified for a state to augment its power only for its own glorification because it certainly invites war and the mere magnification of power is not conducive to the development of the state. Those who are in power possess war inclination — this view represents a pivotal pragmatic point in Kant's war philosophy. War is a reality. In spite of that Kant strongly argues for the prevention of war and the establishment of perpetual peace. Kant condemns the employment of deceitful means in war. This ethical perspective is stressed and glorified also for the establishment of perpetual and future peace because the application of the deceitful means creates distrust among different states which is contrary to the future-peace.

Kant is decisively clear that war should be completely abandoned; hence in his view there is no ethical aspect of war. But as war is a reality, he speaks about its rightful means; otherwise the casualties and devastations of war will be uncontrolled and unlimited. Therefore, in his philosophy, the ethical means of war is for the diminishing of human-sufferings and the confirmation of greater human welfare. Kant opines that only in a civil society war prevention is possible, though the pragmatic reality is that all the conflicts and wars are the subjects to the civil societies as only civil societies contain states, state authority and power. Here, Kant introduces a significant psychological aspect that power involves war inclination. Though it is an empirical fact that all the wars occur only in the civil societies, at the same time Kant expects that civil society alone can ensure war prevention and future-peace. Law prevails exclusively in a civil society and the constraint of law prevents war and conflict, contributes to the preservation of the individual right and freedom and associates/consorts ethics with politics in the society. This conformity between ethics and politics and the respect for the rights of man reduce antagonism between states and ensure peace.

Georg Wilhelm Friedrich Hegel (1770–1831)

In his philosophy, Hegel deals with the concrete life with the concepts of family, civil society and state.

The family is the first moment in "the ethical substance". Love, attachment and feeling unite the members of the family. Civil society is a plurality of individuals, each of whom seeks his own ends and tries to satisfy his own needs. It is an economic organization which involves specialization of labour, institution of law. Family represents universality, civil society represents the moment of particularity and the state represents the unity of the universal and the particular. The state is the culmination of the political dialectical process. Its purpose is to provide the largest and most rationally integrated form of social organization available.

Hegel opines that each state has some relation with other states. The positive relationship between states based on their separateness is called a recognition. Every state has an absolute right to recognition. Every state has a particular interest to stand in a specific relationship with other states — through commerce and diplomatic consultation, because it is also, just like individuals, dependent on other states. The mutual relations between the different states are generally controlled and regulated by the treatises and by the international laws. These require the approval and acceptance by the concerned states. But if this acceptance is withdrawn or refused then ultimately war decides any dispute between the states. Hegel viewed this fact in this way as there was no sovereign body in his time which was more powerful than the individual states and which could take an initiative to solve the disputes among states. A perfect independence of states was unthinkable but there was no social order in which the particular interests of separate states were harmonized amongst each other. This lack of a social order implies that there must be a continuous conflict between the substantial interests of separate states that sometimes needed to be resolved. This is a very pragmatic empirical expression indeed.

The state has to oppose other states when its interests are in danger. It implies that in a resolution of the conflict, that could not refer to the sovereignty of a higher social order, could only be achieved by means of warfare.

War cannot be a goal in itself. Any war should ultimately be a means of restoring a positive and mutual recognition between states. This position on the necessity of war has profound consequences in ethics. Those, who want to fight for the survival of the state, are not merely acting in their own self-interest but do so to defend the interests of the civil society.

In a way, unity of the nation is being expressed with such clarity that the question may be asked whether the unity of the nation might not be caused by war. In a war, self-interest is put aside.

For Hegel, war is not an absolute evil. War is not an unnecessary, random occurrence. It is an essential feature of human history. Hegel admits that war causes injustice, cruelty and waste. But he points out that it has an ethical perspective. War is not a mere external contingent fact. It is a rational necessity. "It is necessary that the finite, property and life, should be posited as contingent. . . ." It is "the condition in which we have to take seriously the vanity of temporal goods and things, which otherwise is usually only an edifying phrase". Here, Hegel's concept of war indicates towards his basic and fundamental philosophical principle which expresses his idea of absolute idealism — that ultimate reality is to be found in what is mental or intellectual, not in what is material. It is to be found, to be specific, in rational thought. Hegel says:

> Everything else is error and gloom, opinion, striving, caprice and transitoriness; the absolute idea alone is being, imperishable life, self-knowing truth, and the whole of truth.

He says that the absolute idea "contains every determinateness" which means that it includes within itself every determinate or distinct thing — every human being, every tree, every star, every mountain, every grain of sand.

Nature and mind are different ways in which its existence is manifested; they are different forms of the absolute idea.

The effect of warfare, is to promote nationalism. "As a result of war, nations are strengthened." The material damages of war are insignificant next to the gains in national unity facilitated through armed conflict. This trades material losses — damages to the state and to society — for ethical gains. War is not an unfortunate accident for Hegel but a necessity of the state — making a state-sustaining process itself. Nationalism requires the existence of more than one nation state. On this basis, warfare becomes the expression of intensification of state identity through violence. This in turn, often gives rise to empire — the expression of the political–economic structures of the state into dependent colonies, with many consequential political advantages. Over and above the material defence of the state, war serves a dual purpose for Hegel. First, it facilitates the formation of unified national consciousness and, second, it permits imperial expansionism, which mitigates many of these socio-economic contingencies directly.

Hegel asserts that in war an individual's moral qualities can be revealed on a heroic scale and war proves the transitory feature of the finite. War is a necessary rational phenomenon. It is the means by which the dialectic of history gets a move on. It prevents the stagnation and preserves the ethical health of nations. It is the chief means by which an individual's spirit acquires renewed vigour or a decayed political organism is swept aside and gives place to a more vigorous manifestation of the spirit. Hegel deals with war as an undeniable fact that characterize human history and reality: instead of simply dismissing this phenomenon as "evil". The major feature of Hegel's philosophy in general is movement. War, for all its tragic consequences brings movement to history and sometimes allows the progress in the consciousness of freedom. Far from being a destroyer of state, war is indispensable to the perpetuation of the state as a social institution. Without occasional recourse to war, the ethical rightness and unity of society would break down and the internal mechanism of the state would concomitantly stagnate.

Hegel's philosophy is a demand for a better world, a world in which the opposition between individual and society would be overcome, a rationally organized world, a world of genuine freedom, a world fashioned to reflect the absolute supremacy of the human mind and its powers of reason. It was the culmination of the historical and philosophical argument of the Hegelian system. It was a dialectical necessity, a synthesis that would have to emerge to reconcile the conflicting elements of the world in which they lived.

Obviously, Hegel had no experience of what we call total war, and he certainly had the Napoleonic wars and Prussia's struggle for independence fresh in his mind. It would be a gross mistake to project back on Hegel our own experience with contemporary wars. When writing in the early nineteenth century, Hegel was not aware of the destructive potential of modern weapons. It is obvious, but it has to be repeated: during Hegel's lifetime, war was violent, of course, but was also very different. Civilians were rarely involved in direct attacks; the powers at war always envisaged the possibility of peace. There were no weapons capable of destroying entire nations and endanger the very survival of human life on earth. Modern warfare is a case in which all members of a state are involved. The violence of modern warfare has become impersonal to a high degree; the machine-gun, that was introduced to the battlefield after Hegel's death, is the modern weapons *par excellence*. In the use of that weapon it is clear that war is a conflict between collective bodies and not individuals.

War is not a completely irrational explosion of violence for him. That is why the concept of nuclear warfare does not fit into this theory. A total and mutual annihilation cannot serve a social and moral purpose, because it does not disrupt self-interest but destroys civil existence. The real conflict of interests between states is not resolved with the means of a total war.

Bertrand Arthur Russell (1872–1970)

Bertrand Russell, discussing his concept of war and peace in his book *Human Societies in Ethics and Politics*, opines that the establishment of a single worldwide authority could make large-scale wars impossible. Considering the post-Second World War scenario Russell speculates that if Russia was completely victorious and occupied a large part of the Western world then it would aggravate the problem and create more bitterness, hate, fear and revengeful attitude. Bringing under control a large and bitterly hostile territory by force leads to terrorism. If a war ends in a draw then there are two possibilities — first, there is a treaty between the states which can establish a hope of peace, though it is temporary and the war may break out again at any moment. Second, the treaty that brings an end to the violence, the blood-shed, and the possibility of the future war; it sharply escalates mutual tolerance and indicates to the end of an ideological strife.

Russell is inquisitive that whether a desirable form of the world government can be established out of the victory of one side. He is quite assured that a war, ends in a draw, can ascertain the future peace by treaties. But the consequences result from the victory of one side are consistent with most stringent test.

Analysing the contemporary situations of Russia and China, Russell says that these two vast powers can occupy any territory for a long time. Russell observes that rivalry of great powers and nationalism are two main causes of conflicts. The victory of one side cannot settle the lasting peace. He is conscious and worried about the tremendous abuses during the war. He believes that his concurrent world may seek peace in the agreement of the East and West and not in the armed force supremacy.

Russell hopes that a world government may be established in the distant feature and for this the consent of the big world powers is essential. If the powerful nations are organized they can create pressure on the small powers for this world government. This end may be achieved without any war, but if war is required it may be waged though it will certainly be very brief and without any horrific experiences of war.

He voices concern over the safety of the world and conjectures/reflects that the outbreak of a Third World War will create much worse situation than the other two world wars. To ward off the possibility of another deadly world war he suggests to abstain from aggressive attitude and pointing out the wickedness of the other side. These two threaten other states with annihilation. Interpreting contemporary world situation Russell remarks that the two remarkable steps of the pacification are keeping antagonistic propaganda against other states under control and allowing other nation to have truthful information.

He cautions against the horrific consequences of another world war which will result in the complete anarchy and destruction of all centers of industry. Russell views the constructive statesmanship as an important initial step that can bring an end to the large-scale wars, provide aid to the suffering and create an environment conducive to a political dialogue that will satisfy the legitimate aspirations of the people.

Russell observes that the contemporary society is closely

related to scientific technique, so the question of its stability is significant. The stability of the scientific society depends on four conditions. First, a single world government and here, Russell highlights on the humanistic attitude, internationalism instead of narrow nationalism. Second, diffusion of prosperity that makes obvious the economic interpretation of war, that the more prosperity of one country can make the other country envious or jealous and can induce it to wage a war. Third, a low birth rate so that the population of the world becomes stable/stationary. Last, the greatest diffusion of power which focuses on that the centralization of power causes war. Without the proper realization of these conditions war is inevitable which will invite anarchy and general lowering of the civilization. Here Russell insists on that a scientifically developed society is not necessarily a highly civilized one. Only a society consists of the scientific techniques with the foregoing conditions can be identified as a civilized society with a high grade. Without this, war will be there and the world will suffer with starvation and death by violence.

Examining and interpreting the contemporary world scenario Russell asserts that Russia always considers hate as the moving force and it creates conflict between Russia and the West. Russia lays an emphasis on the conflict between capitalism and communism and believes that at the end of this struggle communism will be triumphant. Russell condemns this attitude and describes it as a myth which cannot be accepted by the rational thought. It appears that in his contemporary world, economic issues are significant for the creation of war.

Russell has a firm conviction that war is not a solution to the troubles in the world, but conciliation, mutual faith and co-operation may diminish this antagonism. But this conciliation cannot be realized unless and until the conflicting forces believe that safety may be secured through armament.

Russell believes that in his present-day world, Russia and USA are more concerned with the war preparation, i.e. armament, and not with food, clothing, housing, etc. which augments the war possibility and affects the society, disrupts the civilization and in consequence, basic human needs are not fulfilled.

He tries to explain why every nation is anxious or worried about its own safety and security, and why it emphasizes on the armaments to ensure its security. He observes that a low-level rationality works here; each country thinks that the other may attack with a good possibility of victory and so it tries to increase its armaments. So, when the fear of being attacked and defeated rather than the concern about the evils and devastations that the mankind may face due to the war predominates, it causes war.

If each country realizes that it cannot gain something positive by aggression and the other nation will fight only if it is attacked then war possibility may be diminished. Here, Russell thinks that neutral power can play a significant and decisive role. To solve the long-range problems or conflicts Russell points out to the internationalizing of the atomic energy which may prevent the great devastation of the modern war. Decreasing the mutual suspicion and the establishment of the mutual faith and co-operation among different countries can resist war.

Russell repeatedly shows that a world government is required for world peace and so he is against narrow nationalism. He believes that no nation can enjoy anarchic liberty due to the scientific technique in the modern world. For the establishment of an international government, fanatic attitude must be diminished and communities should be viewed scientifically rather than passionately. Scientific spirit which indicates to the judging by evidence and not mere technical developments may significantly contribute to the unification and survival of the world.

Considering the problem of war-prevention Russell delineates a psychological interpretation that the entire human community across the globe commonly shares the capacity for suffering and the human race has the power to reduce this suffering. But this is not possible unless and until the opposite irrational belief can be controlled. The suffering of each and every individual indicates to the failure of the human wisdom and common humanity. Russell hopes that wisdom, human warmth and concrete statesmanship like the affection of parents may undermine the conflict.

Illustrating the relation between reason and passion Russell says that passions or emotions are the only possible causes of our actions. Passion is the regulator and not the cause of action; it denotes to the choice of the right means to an end that one wish to achieve. Evil passions or emotions prevent the actualization of a better world.

Russell advocates that two factors contribute to the irrationality of human beings. First, one may have incompatible desires and he does not wish to realize that they are incompatible. Second, if men are sufficiently irrational, one may be able to induce them to serve his own interests and pretends that they are serving their own. In politics, this type of irrationality is a common practice. Under the influence of excitement irrationality acts well and war is a step in the development of the excitement. War is a subject to the irrational beliefs and desires. War comes up due to the emotions and passions as Russell believes that every action is due to some emotion; but in the case of war this emotion is not regulated by the reason. Strong desire is not contrary to reason. Russell conceives that his dream-world will not be devoid of strong desires; it will consist of constructive emotions like love, friendship, knowledge and arts. Not the strongness of emotions, but the irrationality of emotions causes conflicts and antagonism.

In his opinion good and bad are definable, and these are intimately related to human desires. Passions cause every action and determine its goodness. Reason plays no role here; it is only the slave of the passions. Russell strongly opposed the First World War but he was unable to find out any reason which could justify his own feeling and which could persuade or influence others to pursue an anti-war attitude. It reveals to him that war, a human action is a result of desires and not of reason.

Russell comes to believe that if the entire human race has the same desires and passions, there will be no ethical conflict. But as there is a great difference, the need of ethics comes up to find reasons to persuade a group of people to desire the same things. Ethics is mostly subjective and it is closely associated with politics. Both of these try to ensure collective desires. War breaks out due to the disagreement of desires of different human groups and so war-issue must have a place in the ethical evaluation.

In his book *Why Men Fight*, Russell describes human nature as basically good and suggests that it should be developed without much restrictions. A disciplined growth without constraint brings about creative desires and impulses which is conducive to co-operation among people and it needs a proper educational system. On the other hand, the prevention of the growth gives rise to destructive emotions and impulses which lead to conflict and war.

It shows that war or conflict is closely concerned with the human nature. As it is essentially good, an accurate betterment of it may diminish bloodshed and violence. Russell's concept brushes off war-issue as entirely external socio-political; human mind or nature partially brings forth it.

Democracy, especially liberal democracy, is the best form of government, Russell contemplates. Properly educated people in a democracy are able to drive out destructive impulses of their own as well as of the others which helps in the prevention of war. In democratic scenario individuals have sufficient liberty which contributes to the manifestation of creative impulses and desires. Individual differences and freedom are significant in Russell's philosophy and he prefers such a social order which secures the developments of individual liberty and special individual gifts.

Russell has a sharp criticism of socialism that it sacrifices human values to some narrow and abstract principles. His thought encompasses conspicuous or discernible human value and freedom.

Russell makes a distinction between primary and secondary desires. Secondary desires are the love of power, acquisitiveness, vanity and rivalry which are associated with political activity. These are closely connected with the war concept.

Russell's analysis of the concept of power shows that love of power is a moving force which brings about social changes. War is largely based on this concept of power. Power has two features — it is an infinite desire like love of glory and it takes many forms like energy and none of these is subordinate to other. These make the love of power so troublesome and it helps in the breaking out of war. One nation always remains unsatisfied for this infinite aspect of power and this unsatisfaction provokes it to involve in a war. Its another feature also contributes to conflict and antagonism; one form of power that is wealth of a nation turns into another, say, armaments.

Russell speaks of the special attributes of man like speech, fire, agriculture, writing, tools and large-scale co-operation which distinguish him from the lower animals. Russell observes that man can demand success in all these except in co-operation. Man and animal both possess impulses and desires; but unlike animals man also possesses intelligence of a higher degree which shows him that impulses are often self-defeating and desires can be controlled by intelligence. Intelligence and impulses increase the complexity of social organization and consequently co-operation, diminishing the competition. As there is a conflict between intelligence and impulses, the need of ethics comes up. Russell's view expresses that war is a conflict between intelligence and passions. War breaks out when passions remain triumphant over intelligence. The victory of passions and desires creates more competition than co-operation in the society which destroys the peace-process and provokes war.

Human existence partially depends on human impulses. Though these impulses often inflict disasters upon men but still these are indispensable. Men can live happily with controlled, moderated desires and ethics plays a prominent role here. War or conflict seems to be the obvious result of disorderly or wild human passions.

There are two aspects of human nature — social and personal. Men are partly gregarious as well as partly solitary. If they were completely social like ants or bees, would always think of their society or community and not of their personal impulses. But man has private life and in many respects personal impulses give rise to war. Once more, the society or community of human beings lies within a limited boundary as men belong to some specific state and each state obtains a certain boundary. Hence, in most of these cases, quite naturally, men being unable to consider the entire human community engage in war with other communities to preserve the interests of their own narrow community. Here, being restricted by state circumference, even social perspective of man causes war. Men are distinct from ants in this respect. Like ants, here men are also more concerned with social interests than personal interests and in spite of that, unlike ants, men involve in war with other nations as they have power concept and intelligence. Intelligence, power and desire occasionally convert men into self-tormented species and then men beget war though they are conscious about devastations and sufferings of bloodshed.

Human beings are not only moved by impulses, but also by conscious purposes, and the need of ethics comes here. Ethics distinguishes good purposes from bad ones and also legitimate means from illegitimate ones of achieving them. Russell's observation portrays that both impulses and conscious purposes, bring forth to war. Conscious purposes encompass achieving of more power and wealth, narrow nationalism and so on.

A society with compossible purpose of different individuals or groups certainly will be happier than a society with conflicting ends. A wise social system is one that encourages and cultivates compossible purposes. Conflicting purposes become victorious over compossible ones and give rise to antagonism and war. War seems to be the obvious result of predominant conflicting purposes. Encouraging compossible purposes may help in the phenomenal advances in removing war and conflict.

The impact of the new scientific techniques upon a society creates various complications and problems. The intensification of war is one of the evil consequences of such impact. Earlier societies also faced a number of wars, but the scientific techniques have converted war to an intensified evil in the modern world. This technique has enhanced the powers of rulers and as a result of this, a single individual is creating plans for the whole society. The elementary claims of the individuals are being constantly ignored and to find a way of being rescued from such an evil is a major and severe problem for the present-day world. The ignorance of individual claims and the creation of plans for the whole society by a single individual significantly contribute to the breaking out of war.

In his book *Common Sense and Nuclear Warfare* Russell focuses on the evil and catastrophe of the nuclear war which affects the entire human race and comments that the survival of the whole mankind depends on the prevention of such horrific war. Nuclear war is not only contrary to the interests of some particular nation, class or continent but to the interests of the entire human world. Focusing on the prevention of war from the perspective of the welfare of the entire human race Russell's philosophy expresses humanistic outlook.

Russell closely observes that nuclear warfare is evidently associated with the power-politics which enhances and patronizes such devastating wars. Nuclear warfare is a means of securing victory in war and so power-politics consciously ignores its evil consequences.

Constant fear of the large-scale war causes increasing armaments, increasing expenditure, increasing rigidity of the social structure with diminished liberty. It augments hate and terror in the society. Russell's observation shows that technical advances make war more and more disastrous. Spread of power without wisdom is terrifying and results in war. Russell thinks that human species is self-tormented which inspires it to be involved in a war. The cultivation of hope and benevolence rather than fear and hate is required for the prevention of war. Human beings possess all these emotions. But the predominance of fear and hate over the hope and benevolence creates war. Human desires give rise to war and human desires can prevent it too. The restraint of rivalry not only prohibits evils but helps in the security of immense goods.

Technical advancement may help in the realization of the universal material well-being; but the constant persuasion of rivalry and war contributes to the universal poverty rather than universal prosperity and development.

In the question of negotiation the first and foremost thing is a fresh assessment of national interests of all the powerful states of the world and to enhance the national interests of all the countries concerned. This view expresses Russell's preference of humanistic attitude and his firm stands against narrow-nationalism.

Russell's observation points out that the policy of powerful countries consists of two objects — their prosperity and the political, economic as well as ideological dominion over other states which leads to war and conflict. Russell focuses on the potentialities of scientific warfare in the modern world and comments that a country may be prosperous and secured only by making all other powerful countries safe and prosperous rather than by its dominion over other countries. This is not for any new moral thought but for the modern scientific warfare.

Russell highlights the terrific consequences of the nuclear war which lead to destitute population, hunger, disease, lack of modern industry, transport and education, and he hopes that the powerful countries will be united to prevent war for the sake of their national interests though they conflict over minor issues.

His political view is an obvious constant criticism of narrow nationalism. It is quite natural that a state seeks its own welfare which is not blameworthy at all but when a state tries to be developed at the expense or cost of the welfare of other countries, war and conflict break in. Russell focuses on the psychological aspect for the prevention of war that when each state will be convinced that victory and success cannot be secured through war, they will avoid and abandon war. If both sides have genuine desire for peace without victory for either side war may be prevented.

Russell perceives that reduction of armament is essential for a good economy. New inventions concerning arms race constantly enhances military expenditure of a state. The realization by a state that the prosperity of its own citizen is desirable rather than its ability to kill the people of other countries can resist conflict and related arms race. War implies the involvement of the entire nation which exploits the state power.

Russell argues that fear has to be removed from the mind of all who realize the evil consequences of war. If they fear that they may be killed at any moment then their present lives will be less happy and enjoyable. Civilized world must experience joy and happiness. The energies which are now involved to create hate, devastation and rivalry have to be the source of creativity, happiness and prosperity. Fear originates from war and conflict prevents men from enjoying freedom and hope. So, Russell's philosophy stresses on the prevention of war and disarmament from the utilitarian perspective. Utilitarianism judges actions by their tendency to maximize pleasure or happiness and minimize pain or unhappiness. This doctrine holds that a person that is a self-conscious being has a conception of himself and he knows that he has a future. He also knows that his future existence could be cut short. If he thinks that this is likely to happen at any moment, his present existence will be fraught with anxiety, and will presumably be less enjoyable than if he does not think it is likely to happen for some time. If he realizes that people like himself are very rarely killed, he will worry less. Hence, utilitarianism can defend a prohibition on killing persons on the ground that it will increase the happiness of people who would otherwise worry that they might be killed.

The philosophy of Russell perceives ideological dispute as an obstacle to the installation of peace. When each side firmly believes that its ideology is much better than that of the other and the opposite ideology is of no merit of being triumphant conflict steps in.

War is reprehensible from the humanitarian perspective; its prevention is inevitable. The catastrophe of war has to be viewed and analysed from humanitarian aspect rather than solely from national interest.

Russell points out that an international authority may be established for the prevention of war and the persuasion of peace process. With a well-defined constitution this authority may interfere only for the resistance of war and not for any religious, economic or political cause.

Russell views the conflict between war and peace as the conflict between reason and death. War considers reason as a very feeble force in human affairs.

Human purposes are partly good and partly bad. Whether they are good or bad, their existence depends on the survival of the human race. The non-existence of the concept of good or bad shows that there is no human world. Russell believes that every ideology contains positive as well as some negative aspects and, hence, war cannot be inevitable for the abolition of some ideology which has no good aspect.

Russell's philosophical concept emphasizes on the nationalism as a significant source of war. Nationalism inspires a state to believe blindly in its own excellence over the others and to pursue its own interests even they conflict with those of others. Here, nationalism prevents world unity. But Russell admits the positive contributions of nationalism too. It creates cultural diversities between different states, necessary for literature and art. Nationalism is like an inherent element of human nature and in the modern world it flourishes as a reaction against foreign aggression. Trying to get rid of foreign dominion a nation portrays its own merits and the demerits of the foreign aggressors. At the winning of freedom after the end of struggle this national spirit still continues and the concept of national supremacy provokes that nation for conquest of other states. Russell's analysis shows that though nationalism is a reaction against foreign aggression and dominion, in turn, Russell contemplates, it provokes war.

Russell thinks that for the prevention of deadly wars, system of education of a national state has to be reconsidered and rearranged. In most of the countries state-run education system teaches and inspires something consistent solely with their national interests, and portrays their supremacy and martial glory leading to war.

Russell contemplates war as an obstacle to human progress though in his view past wars against the barbarians to defend the civilization were not blameworthy. Wars, waged at the hands of those who are in the forefront of civilization cause destruction and degradation to the human civilization. This view focuses on that Russell is not a complete pacifist and he believes that some wars are justified. He expresses particular concern over the wars responsible for horrific carnage, devastation and retreat of civilization. His observation is that in the modern world technical and scientific advancements make the victory of either side impossible. Nations involved in war and the neutrals too will be defeated in the present world and points out at the futility of war as an instrument of policy.

Russell's moral view shows conflict between various incompatible desires and emotions as an obvious truth. Change in moral perspective is inevitable with the changing atmosphere of human life. Brushing aside the view to consider groups of human beings other than one's own as possible competitors dynamic global political trends have to deviate away from considering other groups as competitors towards a co-operative outlook. Besides tremendous abuses war tries to quash fundamental rights to life and freedom. People, preferring life to death, are denied their freedom to choose their preference.

Russell describes "good" as the "satisfaction of desires". A thing, satisfying more desires than others, is better than another. "Right" action, influenced by our passions, causes general good. Russell firmly believes that satisfaction of one's desires, bringing dissatisfaction to others, is not good. War involves both victory and defeat. It fulfils the desires of a nation causing dissatisfaction to another. War is not good, Russell holds. Desires, compatible with others are "good" or "right" whereas "wrong" or "bad" desires are mutually incompatible. Good desires are the source of greater total of satisfaction of desires than the bad ones and so they are preferable means. Co-operation is preferable to competition, peace to war. Competition, conflict and war involve incompatible desires and, hence, not the greater total of satisfaction of desires. The desires for victory of the citizens of a nation involves in a war are mutually compossible but they are incompatible with the enemy state. War or competition is not of total satisfaction of desires or general good.

Russell condemns narrow nationalism as it prefers the good of one's own nation and refrains from the consideration of the interests of others. This view — only the good of one race is important — causes war.

Criticizing the doctrine "psychological hedonism" which asserts that every individual should pursue exclusively his own pleasure, Russell comments that this doctrine is wrong in assuming that an individual's desires are limited to what is going to happen to him. His desires are not always the parts of his own experience, but usual to have objects of desire which lie wholly outside his own life. Russell observes that psychological hedonism has a wrong perception that an individual's desires are always for his own pleasure. Human beings not always try to fulfil the desires of their own experience only and this indeed is conducive to the war prevention and peace-process.

Russell's ethical perspective considers the concepts of good and bad as more fundamental than the concepts of right and wrong.

Russell expresses his concern that the complete harmony of private and public interests may be impossible in the practical field. This view is quite contrary to the ancient Indian view of the harmony of individual and social good. In the practical world scenario individual morality or individual good and social morality or social good are not at all compatible; particularly in the case of narrow nationalism. Narrow nationalism provokes a nation or a state to think about its own interests only, even at the expense of other states and such consideration leads to war.

His view clearly delineates that incompatibility between the individual and general good is a prime source of war. The realization, that the true interests of each group are bound up with the general good, is essential for the prevention of war and its evil consequences result in ruins and devastations. Peace process and the restraint of war largely depend on the compatibility of enlightened self-interest and general good. Law and government usually try to ensure an equilibrium between individual good and social good. The abuse of such law and government in the relations between sovereign states prohibits effectively successful equivalence of individual and social good and, hence, war is inescapable.

Russell views war as an outcome of the consideration of a

particular section of mankind as an end and the rest portion merely means. Those, who are being considered as means naturally protest and conflict is assured. Supremacy of a section of mankind contributes to the emergence of endless strifes.

Russell's philosophical reflection shows that every action of man is governed by his desires. Although sense of duty inspires human action but this action involves a desire too — the desire to be dutiful.

Human beings are not only satisfied with the fulfilment of their basic needs like food, shelter, etc. They differ from the lower animals that they possess some infinite desires those keep them restless for ever. Acquisitiveness is one of such desires which is the wish to possess as much as possible of goods and is a combination of fear and desire for necessaries. Those who are more powerful are motivated by this desire certainly and try to acquire as much as possible. Fear of being less powerful and subjugation by others provoke man as well as a nation towards this acquisitiveness and the infinite form of acquisitiveness makes war assured and unavoidable. Rivalry, another infinite desire of the human beings, generates ideological conflicts, ultimately leading to war. Vanity is a motive of immense potency that satisfies the glory of man and such desire for the satisfaction of one's glory contributes to the breaking out of war. Love of power, a significant infinite motive, is increased with the experience of power, Russell thinks. Rulers, enjoying power for a long time possess increasing "love of power" with their experience and they involve in war with the other states to satisfy their love of power. Especially, offensive war comprises of such desires. Those who enjoy love of power generally prefer inflicting pain to permitting pleasure that makes the love of power a dangerous motive. War contains this sort of psychological aspect. Russell, of course, is of the opinion that love of power is not altogether deplorable. The merits and demerits of the actions result from this motive determine its efficacy.

Russell considers fear and hate as two other significant motives of human lives. Man fears something unfamiliar and so hates it. A possible future attack by a foreign country creates fear and in turn generates hate which often leads to war. A foreign country, which is quite unfamiliar, is a potential or actual enemy. A nation with a different and unfamiliar ideology is a source of insecurity that creates fear. Fear, which results from the absence of security, is degrading; it easily becomes an obsession and leads to excessive cruelty.

Russell shows that modern war is profoundly different from the wars of the old days which satisfied the self-interests of the victor parties as they conquered, subjugated their enemies and war was not so much expensive. But in the present-day world, modern techniques have made war expensive and so the human race should refrain from war in their self-interests. Practically a conflict prevails between self-interest and instinct or desire. Though self-interest is concerned with the war prevention, desires like love of power, vanity and acquisitiveness provoke war. Such conflict was not so acute in the old days. Russell's philosophy delineates desires as the cause of every human action and so despite some external reasons war is caused principally by the human desires and impulses.

Industrialism, a source of military power, is a key external cause of war, Russell thinks. Increasing industrialism in the modern world makes war a practical reality and war is intimately related with the industrialism that is the economy of a country. Russell observes that cohesion and rivalry contribute to the military power in a significant way.

Analysing the modern atomic war, Russell comments that atomic energy can be employed in the positive scientific development though war-time exploits it and puts to use in the mutual extermination. Considering man as a "man" and not "separate group of men" is essential for the prevention of the evils result from the war, Russell's humanistic attitude and international consciousness contemplate.

Russell has a firm conviction that increasing scientific skill does not necessarily ensure increasing human happiness. Wisdom is essential for this happiness and mere skill, devoid of wisdom, creates nothing but conflict and war situation in the present-day world.

To avoid the extermination of the human race, the restraint of old crude passions like hate, greed, envy and the expansion of new wisdom are crucial which will help to understand and feel the common danger of the human race that hate creates a reciprocal hate; and it causes finite harm to the individuals though generates infinite and absolute harm to the nations and leads to the complete annihilation of mankind. In the technically developed modern world, co-operation that aims at the good and betterment of the others and not merely of oneself can be the sole way of human survival.

Human happiness is distinct from the happiness of the lower animals. Real human happiness lies in the development of the godlike potentialities. Men, desiring real happiness, feel sympathetic suffering to view the sufferings of others and so, actually, he cannot enjoy real happiness in this modern world.

Russell distinctly points out one crucial psychological aspect of war that human beings find satisfaction and pleasure in the spectacle of suffering. This passion along with others like rivalry, love of power and hate give rise to war. Intelligence of man is giving human passions scope instead of taming them. In the case of war, specially in the field of modern warfare, human intelligence is producing increasing technically developed arms that are much destructive, and provoke and prepare increasing scope for war passions.

Russell's concept of power affirms that power always gives advantage and good things to the strong and leaves misery for the weak ones. Analysing human psychology Russell claims that fiercer passion easily drawing human attraction contributes to the waging war and those who oppose it receive hatred.

In real life, those who encourage destructive passions certainly profit by injustice; though remain completely ignored of the greatest joys of human life and they are bound to curb their more generous emotions. War supporters with destructive attitude possess such mindset.

Russell's political insight observes that conflict between organized passions since the dawn of civilization have been creating antagonism and war that have reduced human happiness. Human beings, employing their intelligence to the creation of such conflict of passions, may assure happiness for a few though lead the majority towards a miserable life. Russell hopes that our passions are not unalterable though human intelligence considers passion so and such conviction/notion is profoundly responsible for the present perilous situation of the world. Alteration of the passions may help the human beings to resist their own evils and destructions, Russell comments.

Russell's philosophical insight delineates that passion rather than reason is the source of all actions. Reason is the slave of passion and war is caused by human emotions. Though emotions effectuate war, not the strongness of emotions necessarily produces it as strongness is not always devoid of reason. War is rather due to the irrationality of human emotions or passions and reason is essential for the prevention of war. Human life involves a natural conflict between passion and intelligence in which, if passion conquers, war breaks in.

The passion or emotion is an integral part of the human existence, when it is uncontrolled war becomes inescapable. War is a result of wild or uncontrolled human passions. Hence, war is intimately concerned with the psychological aspect of man. War is not purely external–socio-political; it is related to the human nature too. Accurate betterment of human nature that is essentially good diminish bloodshed and violence.

Russell conceives that power plays a key role in the emergence of war. Its infinite nature and various forms give rise to antagonism. Power without wisdom is devoid of any ethical and rational constraint and so it is terrific for human existence. Though technical advancement contributes to the material progress, as this advancement is a concept of power with the absence of wisdom as well as rational–ethical constraints it causes competition and rivalry. Prevention of war is closely associated with the constraints of ethical principles. War and ethics are closely interwoven/involved with each other. Disagreement of desires of different human groups invites war and hence the need of ethics comes up to find reason. Men essentially seek their own happiness but occasionally intelligence, power and desire convert them into self-tormented species; despite evils, bloodshed and devastations men involve in wars. Man has both social and individual lives. Personal desires often trigger off war. Even the social aspect of man, when it is limited by state boundary incites war. So, war has psychological as well as social aspects.

Conscious purposes are of two types — compossible and conflicting. Society with predominating compossible purposes rather than conflicting ones may prevent wars.

Russell condemns war on the ground that it is contrary to the right to life and freedom. Culminating creative impulses, adequate liberty or freedom plays a key role in the prevention of war. Hence, Russell views war as the contrary to the right to freedom and freedom resists conflict. Russell stresses on the protection of individual claims, ignorance of which leads to war. His philosophy claims the importance of individual freedom and liberty not only from the perspective of individual interest but for the social stability and peace process.

Rivalry of great powers and narrow nationalism give rise to wars. He condemns aggressive attitude and the tremendous abuses during the war and this expresses his humanistic view. Centralization of power and prosperity bring about war. Hence, war has an economic reason.

Russell in not a complete pacifist. For him war as a protector of civilization is justified. He condemns war when it brings demolition and evils to the human existence which is contrary to ethics and rationality.

In reality, civilized world contains both pleasures and pains. But Russell conceives that a society is civilized in real sense when it is more concerned with happiness rather than sorrow and devastations. So, war, a source of evils and destructions, cannot be a feature of a civilized world. His humanistic view shows that war is against of the interest of the entire human race.

Russell's ethical perspective contains consequential elements. His concepts of good and right are based on the outcomes of actions and he says that good is satisfaction of desires; right action leads to general good. His criticism and evaluation of war are the corollary of the evils and devastations that war brings in. He disapproves war as it is against humanity, human rights and liberty; it is contrary to human happiness and so to human civilization.

Conclusion

The foregoing analysis and discussions transpire that the philosophers engage in a series of intensive inquiries into the relationship between state, society and war.

For Plato, war is an inevitable condition for the maintenance of a luxurious state and so, the justification of war is, thus, for the welfare of the state. This welfare of the state is manifested in the form of desire. Both the offensive and defensive wars aim at the welfare and progression of the state. Originating from the desire for the welfare of the state, the war is a necessity for the society also and the treatment to the enemies should have been done also with the spirit of the welfare of the society.

Plato stresses on the point of the circle of states. The existence of multiple states side by side is one of the main causes of war. Whenever a state longs for its extension, it has to curb it out from another's land. Thus the powerful is always a threat to the weaker one. From this angle of vision Plato arrives to another question. He sees ultimately another element for war in the "desires" which were the most fruitful source of evils both to individuals and to states. But these desires are from the necessity and hence the conduct of war is an art. Plato believes that persons should be well trained in their professions to serve best the society and in his conception each group of people have their own professions. As such, war being the professions of the auxiliaries they should attain efficiency to conduct the war should such situation arise.

Plato contributes also to two ideas which are emboldent in the political history of states at a much later stage of the development of states in the process of history. These two are — the nationalist idea and the international law in the present stage. This nationalist approach and the international law come into question when he deals with the problem if a Greek state being victorious on another Greek state should conduct the pillage in the same manner when a non-Greek state is overpowered. His consideration is here on the basis of race; a Greek and a non-Greek should not have the same treatment from a victor Greek. In this context Plato has drawn a difference between Greek and non-Greek races. He thinks that in wars the treatment of a Greek state in respect of another Greek state which has been defeated should be different than what it ought to be in respect of a non-Greek state. But proceeding from this argument, he reaches to another rationality, because this search is for the justice that there should be some limits and even codes while making treatment to the defeated army and people by the victorious forces. In this discussion he stresses what we call, in the by far later period, international law in respect of war.

Republic searched the root cause of war in the economic necessity and Plato linked the necessity with the idea he expressed in "desire".

Conflict is a common and usual feature of a state (polis) for Aristotle, though not a natural disposition of man, and still a state must be aware of the welfare of the citizens of the other states. So, he generally speaks against war as war violates freedom of the other state.

Aristotle's philosophy supports defensive war and also offensive war only when they are concerned with human welfare. Happiness of the citizens is the prime object of a government and so involvement in an irrational conflict is unjustified. Unnecessarily, aggressive war defies law and justice essential for human happiness and welfare. Rule devoid of justice is detrimental to human welfare, and provokes domination, tyrannizes others and leads to war. A state is originated and exists for the satisfaction of bare needs of life and for the sake of a good life; aggressive irrational war defies that good life. An emerging obstruction in the political life, war denounces real and true happiness. War is not a natural disposition of man.

Aristotle speaks both in favour and against war on the same deliberation — welfare of the human beings — from two different perspectives. War is for the good and benefit of the people, and it causes their ruins and devastations too. Certainly war involves catastrophe and destructions, but while it encompasses greater horizon of human welfare it is defensible. Happiness is the end of human nature, it is an activity rather than a disposition. Happiness is an activity that is desirable in itself and not desirable for the sake of something else; for it does not lack anything, but is self-sufficient. The happy life is virtuous and happiness lies in virtuous activities. Military actions aim at an end and are not desirable for their own sake. When they aim at the restoration of human happiness that is the end of human nature, they are defensible.

Aristotle's theory of war may be termed as consequential principle, in a different form. War is good or evil for its consequences. Consequences may be a union of both good and evil — both the welfare and ruins of the people simultaneously where larger welfare than ruins justifies war. War cannot be purely good, but for the good, prosperity and happiness of the citizens war is justified.

War originates from desires. Good, rational desire involves law and justice, leads to good consequences with a non-aggressive view.

Locke holds that aggressive war denies right to life, liberty and possession of others that is unjustified though he speaks for defensive war as an empirical reality to restore law, rational consideration, equality, liberty with a limited passion. Self-preservation justifiably reveals the necessity of defensive war. War is an evil outcome of uncontrolled desire and narrow self-interests. In self-defence killing is justified. Defensive war is the war against injustice for the protection of life and property. Defensive conflicts both in the lives of individuals and the states are permissible. Law of nature sanctions defensive conflict and social laws are also conducive to it.

Kant condemns war as it is incompatible with human peace, liberty, right and equality, and it imposes an unnecessary economic burden on the concerned states. Law rather than war is the rational means to solve the international disputes. Power concept and desire to be a supreme power cause aggressive war with the principle "might is right" that is contrary to rational consideration, law, justice and perpetual peace. Power has a natural warlike inclination that sparks off war with a favourable circumstance. The glorification and prosperity of a state do not consist in mere power. War or possession of other state is not at all conducive to culture and tradition.

Kant opposes war, but as it is a practical reality he stresses on the ethical perspective of war and its fair means to associate politics with ethics. True concepts of right and freedom, and the formation of a world community can resist war inclination by establishing justice. Vested interests of men incite war. Motivated by the desire of being prosperous a state power involves in a war which in turn defies its prosperity by severely weakening its financial and commercial basis. Rational consideration, respect for law, justice, freedom and rights of men, and the association of politics with ethics may diminish global war scenario.

Kant views that desire for power and self-interest give rise to aggressive war. Kantian philosophy considers good-will as the highest good and the condition of all other goods. An act is good only when it is out of good-will and motivated by duty. War in its aggressive form has no motivation of duty, it is certainly indefensible. Defensive war has an end of happiness related to law and justice. Kant argues that happiness cannot be the ultimate purpose of morality. Fortune, power, courage and happiness can be used to bad ends though they are known as traditional virtues. Neither aggressive nor defensive war is out of only sense of duty but with some purpose or interest as the end. So, war is totally denounced from Kantian morality, rational criticism rather than war or rebellion is appropriate/decorous for a solution of conflicting issues. Amidst his fierce ethical resistance to war, both aggressive and defensive, Kant accepts the practical reality of war and hence he speaks of the ethical constrains on war.

Hegel shows that the existence and mutual relations between the various states of the world are determined by different treatises and international laws that need the consents of the concerned states, the negation of which brings on war. A state declares war for the protection of its citizen's interests and so war involves desire — desire for the happiness of the people — prevention of the severe weakening of the nation, internally and externally, and for the prevention of the economic devastation.

War is not an end in itself. Defending welfare, stability and progress of the society it acts as a means, not satisfies self-interest of a particular individual or group. Like Plato and Aristotle, Hegel views desire as the origin of war — an elevated desire of preserving prosperity and unity of a nation. Amidst its consequential devastations and cruelty war is a rational necessity. War is not for the self-interest of some particular individuals, but for the entire society. The progression of the society naturally allows progression of its different individuals that may reduce the opposition between the two.

Notion of right has a key place in Hegel's moral concepts. A person has an inalienable right to life and to freedom and to a minimum of personal property. Society alone can protect these rights and provide a context for individual human flourishing. Rights are essential as an individual can only express himself as a free spirit by providing himself an external sphere of freedom. A right is an entitlement to property interpreted in a broad sense for Hegel, one's body, life and liberty are his property like material things. Society protects the rights of the individuals and for the preservation of that society war is inevitable. A good purpose is required for an action to be morally good. With a good purpose of stabilizing the society for the sake of individual rights makes war good. As a rational necessity, war is not an aggressive war that claims innocent civilian lives.

Russell also indicates that desire or passion provokes war while it is uncontrolled and without any rational reflections. Power devoid of wisdom has no moral perspective and it exaggerates irrational emotions that invite bloodshed. War is incompatible with human liberty that is inevitable not only for individual interest but for the social peace and stability. War cannot be a feature of a civilized world as it brings destructions and pains, and civilized society contains more happiness than pains. War is a practical truth that originates from socio–economic–psychological perspectives. For social peace and stability Russell prefers and advocates a humanistic and non-aggressive view of war as the entire negation of violence and bloodshed is inconceivable.

Here, a striking similarity as well as a contrast is worth to mention between Russell's view and the Indian concept of war. Both are quite unambiguous that human beings are making themselves their own enemies by waging wars. Both stress on controlled desires though from different perspectives. Indian concept holds that desire is a cause of war; but it should be controlled. War with a controlled desire does not lead to aggressive war. On the other hand, Russell says that passions lead to war when it is uncontrolled.

So, the Indian concept stresses on controlled desires first for resisting war, and following *sāma, dāna, bheda* principles, and second, if war is to be pursued for the benefit of the state then it must be with controlled desires so that devastations may be lessened. In Russell's view, war has no relation with controlled desires, but with uncontrolled one. Russell's view holds that men can live happily with his controlled desires and war has no capacity to make a man happy.

Indian concept points out that following the failures of *sāma, dāna, bheda* principles, as a last resort when a war is pursued for the welfare of the state, it must be with controlled desires. This war is for the development and prosperity of a state, very essential for its existence and hence it increases happiness of its subjects. Indian concept is certainly aware of the devastations of a war, and so its prescribed principles of war and the post-war attitude are for the reduction of horrendous casualties of war.

Both Russell and the Indian authorities believe that controlled desires are conducive to happiness but at the question of war, they differ. War as a last resort with controlled desires aims at the welfare of the subjects of a state whereas Russell's ethical perspective has no place for war.

Devastation, annihilation, death and casualties form the area of concern of all philosophers for almost 2,000 years. Amidst that, except Kant, all extend their support to war for the preservation of social order and the restoration of peace and justice though that war has to be non-aggressive, rational and mostly defensive in nature. Whereas Kant finds no crucial rational element in war and war is altogether denounced and condemned in his perspective. To him, critical rational discussion and criticism rather than war is capable of restoring peace and justice and restarting social stabilizing process.

War is a practical reality and so they advocate the principle of "live and let live" denoting a process of reciprocal exchange among antagonists, where each diminish the other's risk of death, discomfort and injury but a deliberate restriction of aggressive activity, but only on condition that the other requires the restraint. This principle and mutual empathy reduce the horrors of war though not altogether eradicate it from this world.

5

A Synthesis
Indian and Western Perspectives and a Reflection on the Present-day War

BOTH the Indian and Western thinkers consider desires — desires for power, stability, wealth, prosperity and happiness — as the origin of war. Aggressive war should be denounced. In self-defence, defensive war is permissible. For the protection of society, individual freedom, equality and rights defensive war is essential. Defensive war allows the employment of force as a necessary fact though it declares that there are limits to when one is liable to use this necessary force as a means of self-defence. The authorities stress on the proportionality of level of defensive force to the threatened harm. Defensive force must be proportionate to the permissible defence. War is a "last resort" for them (although Hegel supports war gracefully and Kant condemns war altogether), so it has a necessity condition that prohibits one from applying more force than one has to in defence. The right-based account of self-defence explains that the right not to be killed is a claim right that imposes on others a duty of non-interference and a duty of assistance. Duty of non-interference confirms that one has to refrain from interfering with such right while as duty of assistance refers to one's obligation to contribute to the fulfilment of that right.

One has no right to kill the other and he has a duty not to kill him. But if he attacks or tries to kill someone else he violates his duty and the right of the other not to be killed. As he proceeds to violate other's right; he lacks the right that the other not kills him and the other will not violate his right by killing him. For this reason, killing the soldiers of the invading state is justified though not the innocent civilians as they do not lack their right not to be killed. Non-combatants are not part of the invading army.

The soldiers of the invading state are liable to defensive killing as they are morally responsible for an unjust threat. A unjust threat is a threat of harm that will wrong the person upon whom it is inflicted: it is a threat of harm directed at a person who is not liable to that harm. A state wages a defensive war to protect the rights of its citizens to live and to live a manner they like. So, defensive war is conducive to the rights of the individuals.

Philosophers perceive war as the last resort and modern thinkers mostly propose a world organization to solve the conflicting issues of different states to avoid war.

There is a difference between morality and law. Law is devised by humans. Law has a purpose in a way that morality does not have. It can be altered and shaped to meet human ends, because it is humans who determine what the law is. On the other hand, morality cannot be altered as it does not suit our purposes. It exists independently of our ends. The Indian and Western political thinkers (both ancient and modern) advocate that the laws of war do not diverge from morality, but correspond with it while they propose non-combatant immunity in war. It is a tragic, but inescapable feature of war that the innocents are killed along with the guilty. The law protecting all non-combatants from intentional attack is the morally best law that does not conflict with morality. The soldiers of the invading state fight not as individual but as representatives of their state. Soldiers rather than the civilians have collective identity. Civilians, on the other hand, being also the members of the enemy nation, are identified as individuals. Soldiers are part of a guilty collective and they are identified as nation's agency. One state can attack and kill the combatants of the invading state in self-defence as they are part of a guilty collective, even if they are morally innocent as individuals. It transpires that morally unjust and prohibited rule in the case of individual may be just and permissible while it is employed in the sphere of collective army.

All of them justify defensive war (though Kant does not do so explicitly) for the welfare and development of the state. The welfare of the state means the welfare of the citizens the state is comprised of. State is there for the sake of its citizens. Here individual right and prosperity are compatible with collective welfare.

Both Indian and Western ancient philosophers emphasize on the cause of war — rather on the just cause of it, that inevitability brings on war and war is here inescapable. For the ancient Indian philosophers war is a *dharma-yuddha*, it is essential for the social stability and justice. It is illegitimate to abstain from such war irrespective to chance of success. In the modern age, both India and West realize the significance of war for the stability, progression and development of state; re-establishing of equality, liberty and justice that turns war a duty for the state authority. Just cause, rather than chance of success or failure prevails prominent and transparent in the thought-horizons of modern philosophers (both from Indian and Western world).

In the very recent contemporary world of political thought, a reasonable chance of success is manifested as a glorious condition for a just war. May be this is so as in the contemporary wars the leaders of the states usually do not directly take part like previous-age rulers though they take the decisions of such violence and bloodsheds. Without considering the chance of success sending army to warfront is unjustified and irrational slaughter that is not permissible. This aspect of recent wars leads to the acceptance of reasonable chance of success as a justified requirement along with its just cause. The justification of war not solely lies in the protection of the life, land and sovereignty; lies with the very fact that the non-occurrence of war allows the aggressive country to devastate the common life and that common life is the pre-condition of the protection of life, liberty and land. Just war aims at the resistance of the humanitarian abuses.

Indian and Western thinkers acknowledge specific rules of war to decrease the number, horrors and aggression of war.

Realism is a theory that denies the necessity of such rules in a war. State leaders aim at their national interests, augmentation of power and security in a war and the moral rules are not conducive to these ends. They argue that the absence of rules is good and beneficial for the warring states from the consequential point of view. War triggers off violence, brutality, bloodshed and casualties. Rules of war prolongs war and give rise to much more violence and casualties than if the war occurs without any moral constraint that makes it short though brutal. Moreover, realists believe that the nature of war and humanity defy the possibility of restraining people's actions in what are the most dire situations that mankind can imagine. But practically, combatants generally follow and observe the rules of war. In recent time, a distinction is emphasized between the professional soldiers and the terrorists that the former fight in an honourable way respecting rules of war.

It is a fact that modern warfare is often remote, employing

unmanned aircraft and long-range weaponry. Wars are fought by the well-equipped and well-trained standing armies. But all these do not transpire that war does not require rules of war and the warriors are not willing or capable of being guided by these rules.

Ancient and modern authorities repeatedly reflect on the importance of the rules of war and its moral aspect for protecting the innocent citizens, heritage and culture and for reducing aggression.

Another contentious issue concerning the rules of war focuses on a really very hard question that whether the combatants are capable of fighting justly an unjust war or not. This issue originates from a perception that a just war may be unjustly fought and an unjust war be justly fought. Waging war is a decision solely taken by the state leaders or state authority and they are morally and legally responsible for the justness of that war and so it is a political matter. The soldiers just obey the orders of their state authority to fight a war — whether it is just or unjust — and they have no control over the sort of war. The combatants only have the control on the military aspect of a war — the rules of war — the rules by which the war is fought. Following rules properly in the warfront they may fight legally and justly an unjust war.

Ancient and modern views on war do not have conformity with the foregoing concept. They contemplate that the justness of a war is essentially determined by its source or reason. War waging for the prosperity, development of the state and not for any personal interest of the ruler; non-participation of which generates evils and instability for society leading to its destruction is a just war. Again, rules of war are prescribed to diminish violence, brutality and aggression in war and to protect the innocent civilians. These constitute the essence of a just war, devoid of which a war cannot be just. While a war is just, both its political and military aspects have to be just; the actions of both the state leaders and the combatants in the warfront are to be just. The leaders and the combatants — both contribute to the justness of a war as both are the integral parts of the war scenario.

Traditional concept of just war principle that it needs a legitimate authority to declare and fight is reflected throughout the war theory of Indian and Western authorities (both ancient and modern). War is a reality as there are many states and who represents the state as well as speaks for the state in the international sphere is the legitimate authority. In recent world scenario this concept demands an observation and reassessment as wars are increasingly effectuated against some non-state organizations like terrorist groups (e.g. Al-Qaeda) and ethnic or religious groups in civil wars (e.g. Liberation Tigers of Tamil Eelam in Sri Lanka) rather than state powers. Contemporary wars are not always the conflicts between two appropriate state authorities, but against non-state groups too.

Traditional philosophers (both Indian and Western) speak not only of just cause but right intention too for a just war. Right intention is a just cause that is also morally appropriate. When a war is generated and applied a just cause not to protest a wrong reason, but rather for some other political and economic purposes it can be condemned for not having a right intention.

In contemporary world, the state leaders do not take part directly in the battlefield and they send their soldiers to fight. Here, the state authority has no right to sacrifice the lives of their combatants in a fight that is without a right intention. In the present world "right-intention" principle of a just war is quite relevant. In the recent past the world viewed a deviation from such principle when Britain and USA declared war against Iraq in 2003 demanding with a just cause to locate the weapons of mass destructions in Iraq though in reality with a reason to make an easy access to oil field and to dethrone the regime. The war was portrayed as a war against the wrong reason while actually it was a war for several other reasons.

Both ancient and modern political thinkers (Indian and Western) acknowledge the "last resort" as a feature of a just war. They realize the necessity of a war while it is a last resort for the protection and stability of a state's sovereignty. When all the other ways to avoid war exhaust, war is the only reality. This feature emphasizes on the resistance and avoidance of an unnecessary war and it has actually no role to play while a war is already sparked off.

Present world also recognizes this "last resort" feature of war and state power tries to avert war through some other alternative measures like diplomatic pressure, negotiation, economic sanctions, trade bans and UN Security Council resolutions.

Ancient and modern philosophers (both in the Indian and Western fields) mostly perceive war as defensive war. In case of the assaults by the invaders causing serious threat to the integrity and security of the country, waging of war against the invaders is considered as essential and just. This war causes good to the state.

Ancient Indian thinkers also speak of the conquest of a new territory because they believe that possessing unacquired lands is a duty of a king and it is beneficial for his subjects. The protection of the acquired lands as well as the possession of unacquired ones is considered as a king's duty by them. A king needs to engage himself to succeed righteously in a battle and to add riches to his treasure though such offensive measure is conducive to the defensive purpose. Arrangement for proper defensive measures of his country and the happiness of the people — the prime task of the king — requires a rich treasure and for that the king should have the desire to conquer and have wealth.

Defensive war as portrayed by the ancient and modern philosophers is a punitive war and the waging of that war is an act of punishment after an attack. Justification of punishment here reflects on two aspects — restriction that aims to restore and re-establish justice by punishing the invaders and deterrence for discouraging both the invaders and others from causing future aggressive wars.

In present-day world this punitive aspect of war is not being profoundly acknowledged as justified though in recent past, world viewed a punitive war after the First World War in the disarming of Germany to resist Germany from another future aggression. On two grounds the justification of punitive war is being undermined in the contemporary thought. First, there is no proper authority to take the punitive measure. A state is the appropriate authority that can adjudicate between its citizens but there is no such authority that can adjudicate between states. So, there can be no justified punishment of one state by another. Though UN contains representatives from almost all countries of the world, UN is not an impartial democratic organization, rather its decisions are being extensively influenced by the interests of its five permanent members who have veto rights. Second, present world thinks that punitive war is unjust as it does not fulfil the principle of discrimination that making a distinction between the guilty and the innocent declares that to punish the innocent for the guilty of others is morally impermissible. Punitive war inevitably inflicts harm on the guilty as well as the innocent people though the combatants try to follow the rules of war carefully. Punishing those who are not guilty along with those who deserve it is certainly unjust.

This principle of discrimination plays a key role in the ancient and modern thought-spectrum and the protection of the lives and rights of the innocent civilian people is enormously emphasized. The recognition of this principle is reflected through their non-aggressive views of war.

Ancient authorities distinctly confirms that state is the appropriate and justified body that deserves the right to declare war (both defensive and offensive) and that war is solely for the development, prosperity, sovereignty of the state and its citizens, and not for the personal interest of the ruler. Some modern thinkers reveal the necessity of an international organization that may contribute to the diminishing of conflicts and bloodsheds though unlike the present-day thinkers they consider state as possessing the power of announcing war, making treaties and endeavouring for peace.

Non-combatant immunity is a key and central idea in the ancient and modern war concepts. A distinction is maintained between combatants and non-combatants, and the right to life is viewed as a basic right of all — irrespective of combatant or non-combatant people. At wartime, non-combatants do nothing that can forfeit their right to life and hence, intentional killing of non-combatants is unjust though it is true that some innocent civilians are incidentally killed.

Present thinkers too perceive this issue as crucial for war theory. Attacking other people soldiers forfeit their rights to life. Combatants are instruments both to their commanders and enemy and so their kiling is permissible.

Some current thinkers argue that being the proximate cause of war or threat soldiers are the permissible targets of defence. While two or more agents cause unjust threat with moral responsibility, the agent whose action is the last in the causal chain is the proximate cause of the threat.

Non-combatants may have moral responsibility for a war or may contribute to wartime threat. But they are remote threats, not proximate ones, so are not liable to intentional killing.

Present view on war morality conceives the relation between the citizens and their army that the citizens employ the soldiers to fight for them, to take risks for them and to be targeted instead of them. That is their job, they accept that they are legitimate targets and they accept this to avoid the possibility of being the civilians targeted.

Recently developed war theories also reveal that the non-combatant immunity issue is a mere conviction that originates with the desire to diminish the bloodshed and casualties of war. Non-combatant immunity is not a moral principle independent of any actual convention or practice. There is moral reason not to kill non-combatant in war but convention incites that reason and the issue is a "convention-dependent obligation".

Ancient and modern thinkers, on the other hand, view the non-combatant immunity as a purely moral principle that aims at lessening violence and casualties.

A very recent theory believes that not only the combatants are morally responsible for unjust threat and are the legitimate targets, civilians also provide help and support to the war and play a significant political role in bringing the war on and so like the army they can be legitimately killed too in a war. Amidst this possibility, this theory expresses its concern over the disproportional element that intentionally killing the civilians exceeds the scope of their liability.

Despite all these contentious issues present world recognizes the intentional killing of non-combatants as a war crime. The violation of this principle is generally punished internally by one's own military organization. A soldier accused of intentional killing of civilians usually face a court martial rather than a criminal trial. There are also cases where combatants are tried by criminal courts, such as the trial of Trooper Kevin Williams for the murder of an Iraqi civilian in

2003. Large-scale violations of this principle sometimes make it a subject matter under the jurisdiction of the International Criminal Court.

Ancient and modern philosophers and the recent thinkers too believe that a war is not a just war without justice after war, re-establishing peace and reconstruction. The recent conflicts in Iraq and Afghanistan spark off the debate about the justice after war as an ethical issue. The way of ending a war and the justice after war essentially contribute to the justness of a war. Despite having just cause and rules, a war may be undermined as just without justice after war.

Current war concept distinguishes minimalist approach from maximalist one concerning post-war attitude of a victor state. Minimalists consider "justice after war" as permissions that prescribe the victor nation what it is allowed to do at the ending of war. This principle restricts the post-war attitudes of the conquering state and it is contrary to the notions that the enemies have to surrender unconditionally and the victors possess the right to acquire whatever they like from the vanquished people. Minimalist account emphasizes on the protection of the human rights of the conquered ones and so denies the enslavement of the defeated ones and the colonialization of the defeated land though the temporary occupation of the land is permissible for the protection, recovery and reconstruction. The essence of this minimalist view is also clearly manifested in the war concepts of the ancient and modern authorities.

A more recent idea in this sphere is the maximalist approach. It portrays the "justice after war" as an obligation imposed upon the conqueror rather than permission. Their concern originates from the notion that the victor state usually does little for the vanquished land that leads to the wants of its citizen's basic needs.

The idea "justice after war" recognizes combatants as distinguished from the innocent civilian people who are not responsible for the war and so are not liable to punish. The imposing financial penalties are not to be so severe that defy the right to life and live of the common people that were the case in Germany after the First World War.

It is decisively clear that the current world is confronting N-danger or the fear from nuclear weapons. Recent observation and analysis reveal that 1,600 tonnes of weapons-grade Highly-Enriched Uranium (HEU) and 500 tonnes of plutonium exist in the world, sometimes stored under questionable security. Just the smallest amount of plutonium — about the size of an apple — could kill hundreds of thousands and spark a global crisis. Only about 20 kg of HEU or 8 kg of plutonium would be required to build a working nuclear bomb. There are many other radioactive sources such as nuclear power plants, research facilities and hospitals, which, store isotopes used in treating cancer and other conditions. Experts say this material could be used by terrorists to spread contamination through a "dirty bomb". International Atomic Energy Agency (IAEA) has confirmed twenty cases of theft or loss of HEU or plutonium in the past two decades and hundreds more cases of other radioactive material going missing. In March 2012, US president Barack Obama joined the leaders of more than fifty countries in Seoul, South Korea, for a nuclear security summit meeting, where fears about two rogue states, North Korea and Iran, loomed over a gathering ostensibly about perils of nuclear terrorism. The US president voiced concern over safety of Pakistan's nuclear arsenal too. It transpires that the provocations and pursuit of nuclear weapons by different states have not achieved the security they seek, rather have undermined it. Instead of the dignity, they desire, they will be more isolated. In the current scenario, it is better to respect nations than to scare them and colonize them. The time of imperialism has long gone. Those who do not learn from the mistakes of history will be punished.

War is a hard practical reality in the present world, and the extensive spectrum of conflicts and violence establishes that reality. Balkan country's brutal 1992-95 war killed 100,000 people and left 2.2 million homeless. Interventions in Iraq and Afghanistan by USA in the recent past and the still ongoing civil wars and uprisings across the countries in central Asia and Africa like Syria, Egypt, Tunisia, Baharin, Lybia have delivered an electrifying message — an old order can be ousted. These countries are the spectators of horrific carnage, violence and bloodshed. The Arab spring toppled the dictators in Egypt, Tunisia, Lybia and catalyzed pro-democracy demonstrations in other countries too with a horrific experience of war and tremendous abuses during the war.

These uprisings are the reactions against evil administrative practice, stagnant political situation, immoral economy, unfair election process, inflation, dire poverty, absence of promising jobs and industries, proper education and health. In these countries, autocratic regimes prevailed for a considerable long tenure that followed repressive measures and violated basic human rights of the people. In Egypt, autocrat Hosni Mubarak declared emergency law since 1967 and curbed individual rights and liberty. The desires to restore, re-establish and defend these rights trigger off the popular uprisings. Ancient, modern and contemporary war philosophies are well reflected through these world events that desire causes war and conflicts. These uprisings have right intentions and in their non-occurrence the rights and liberties of the citizens would not be regained and protected. Again, the desire for establishing democracy accelerates the civil wars. Democracy is required for the identification and promotion of the human rights that are preconditions for a good life. Autocracy puts a great challenge before the growth and development of human rights. The compatibility of the concepts of human rights and democracy is beyond doubts as democracy creates the basic conditions for flourishing human rights, and human rights constitute the inalienable and inviolable rights of individuals that can be developed and enjoyed properly in a democracy. All these Asian and African countries are passing through the civil wars of defensive nature from the perspectives of their right intentions and just cause though these are devoid of right rules of war and possess an aggressive feature of massive violence and sense of retribution. These uprisings are the important initial steps that could bring an end to the oppressive autocratic rules, provide aid to the sufferings, and create an environment conducive to a political dialogue that would fulfil the legitimate aspirations of the citizens. Still with their aggressive nature, horrific violence and horrendous casualties — contrary to the proper rules of war — may not be viewed as just and dignified by the ancient and modern authorities.

Bibliography

Andrews, C.F., *Mahatma Gandhi's Ideas*, Macmillan India, 1930.

Aurobindo, Sri, *The Ideal of Karmayogin*, Pondicherry: Aurobindo Ashram, 1913.

Aurobindo, Sri, *The Human Cycle, etc.*, Pondicherry: Aurobindo Ashram, 1952.

Aurobindo, Sri, *The Doctrine of Passive Resistance*, Pondicherry: Aurobindo Ashram, 2002.

Bandyopadhaya, Manabendu, *Manu Saṁhitā*, Calcutta: Sanskrit Pustak Bhandaram 1986.

Berki, R.N., *The History of Political Thought: A Short Introduction*, London: J.M. Dent & Sons, 1977.

Bilimoria, Purushottama, Joseph Prabhu and Renuka Sharma, *Indian Ethics; Classical Traditions & Contemporary Challenges*, New Delhi: Oxford University Press, 2008.

Brown, Chris, Terry Nardin and Nocholas Rengger, *International Relations in Political Thought*, Cambridge: Cambridge University Press, 2002.

Clark, Ian, *Waging War: A Philosophical Introduction*, Oxford: Clarendon Press, 1988.

Coker, Christopher, *Human Warfare*, London: Routlege, 2001.

Copleston, Frederick, *A History of Philosophy*, vols. 1, 6, 7 and 9, London: Continum, 2003.

Datta, Rameshchandra, *R̥gveda Saṁhitā*, Kolkata: Haraf Prakashani, 1976.

Frowe, Helen, *The Ethics of War & Peace: An Introduction*, London & New York: Routledge, 2011.

Ghosal, U.N., *A History of Indian Political Ideas*, Oxford: Oxford Unversity Press 1959.

Ghosh, B.N. and Monika Singh, *Politics and Economics of the Gulf War*, New Delhi: Deep and Deep Publications, 1991.

Ginsberg, Robert (ed.), *The Critique of War: Contemporary Philosophical Explorations*, Chicago: Henry Regnery Company, 1969.

Godbole, V.S., *Rationalism of Veer Savarkar*, Thane: Itihas Patrika Prakashan, 2004.

Griffith, Ralph T.H., *The Hymns of the Rgveda*, Delhi: Motilal Banarsidass, 1973.

Hamton, Jean, *Political Philosophy*, Delhi: Oxford University Press, 1998.

Hume, David, *Essays: Literary, Moral and Political*, New York: Cosmo, 1903/1904.

Kant, Immanuel, *Perpetual Peace: A Philosophical Essay*, New York: Cosimo, Inc., 2010.

Kant, Immanuel, *Political Writings*, ed. H.S. Reiss, tr. H.B. Nisbet, Cambridge: Cambridge University Press, 1991.

Kenny, Anthony, *The Rise of Modern Philosophy*, vol. 3, Oxford: Clarendon Press, 2006.

Law, N.N., *Studies in Ancient Hindu Polity*, London: Longmans, Green and Company, 1914.

Lebow, Richard Ned, *Why Nations Fight*, New York: Cambridge University Press, 2010.

Mahapatra, Anandikumar, *Bharatiya Rashtradarshan*, Kolkata: Suhrid Publication, 1998.

May, Larry, *War Crimes & Just War*, New York: Cambridge University Press, 2007.

Miller, David, *Political Philosophy, A Very Short Introduction*, Oxford: Oxford University Press, 2003.

Nardin, Terry, *Ethics of War & Peace: Religious and Secular Perspective*, Princeton, New Jersey: Princeton University Press, 1998.

Nathanson, Stephen, *Terrorism & the Ethics of War*, New York: Cambridge University Press, 2010.

Norman, Richard, *Ethics, Killing and War*, New York/Melbourne: Cambridge University Press, 1995.

Nozick, R., *Anarchy, State and Utopia*, New York: Basic Books, 1974.

Ojha, Kirtivas, *Rāmāyaṇa*, Kolkata: Paschimbanga Nirakkharata Durikaran Samity, 1974.

Plato, *The Republic*, tr. W.H.D. Rouse, New York: Mentor, 1956.

Priyadarshi, P., *India's Contributions to the West*, New Delhi: Standard Publishers, 2004.

Radhakrishnan, S., *An Anthology*, ed. A.N. Marlow, London: George Allen and Unwin, 1952.

Radhakrishnan, S., *Is This Peace*? Bombay: Hind Kitab Publishers, 1945.

Raphael, D.D., *Problems of Political Philosophy,* 2nd edn., New York: Palgrave, 2009.

Roy, Krishna (ed.), *Political Philosophy: East & West,* Kolkata: Centre of Advanced Studies in Philosophy, Jadavpur University in collaboration with Allied Publishers, New Delhi, 2003.

Russell, Bertrand, *Common Sense and Nuclear Warfare,* London: George Allen & Unwin, 1959.

———, *Human Society in Ethics and Politics,* London and New York: Routledge Classics, 2010.

Sen, Amartya, "History & the Enterprise of Knowledge", Inagural Address, Indian History Congress: 61st Session, Kolkata, 2001.

Sen, M.L., *The Rāmāyaṇa of Vālmīki,* Delhi: Munshiram Manoharlal, 1978.

Shamasastry, R., *Kautilya's Arthaśāstra,* Mysore: Mysore Printing & Publishing House, 1960.

Singh, Gyanender, *Indian Political Thinkers,* New Delhi: Omega Publications, 2008.

Sinha, Kaliprasanna, *Mahābhārata*, Kolkata: Tulikalam, 1987.

Soni, Suresh Kumar, *Human Rights,* New Delhi: Regal Publications, 2012.

Varma, V.P., *Modern Indian Political Thought,* Agra: Laksmi Narain Agarwal Educational Publishers, 2006.

Index